C O N T E N T S

COLOR THE ROUTE
FROM YOUR HOMETOWN TO CHICAGO

If you're flying, color the states you'll fly over.
If you're driving, color the states you'll drive through.
If you live in Chicago or Illinois, color the states you have visited.

1 WELCOME TO CHICAGO!

Where can you find great deep dish pizza, towering skyscrapers, and a lake that looks as big as an ocean? Hold on to your hats—it's time to visit the Windy City, otherwise known as Chicago.

Stroll down Michigan Avenue on a breezy day and you may think you've figured out why Chicago is called the Windy City. Although many people believe the fierce wind is the reason for this nickname, Chicago is actually called the Windy City because of its politicians. In the 1800s a New York City reporter called Chicagoans "windy" because they liked to brag about their city. And as you'll soon find out, Chicagoans have lots to brag about.

⇧ **Bronze lions adorn the front of the Art Institute of Chicago.**

SECOND TO NONE CITY

Although New York, Boston, and Philadelphia were already bustling towns when Chicago was still a swampland, Chicago caught up quickly. It's now the third largest city in United States, right behind New York City and Los Angeles. Three of the nation's tallest skyscrapers—the Sears Tower, the John Hancock Center, and the Standard Oil Building—are all located here. So is the world's largest grain market, as well as the world's busiest airport, O'Hare International. Buckingham Fountain, one of the world's largest fountains, displays its dazzling colors all summer long. And if you felt like reading for the rest of your life, you could check out over 2 million books at the Harold Washington Library, right in the heart of the city.

Chicago has many nicknames, including the Windy City, the City That Works, the Second City, the City of Parks, and the City of Big Shoulders.

⬆ **Chicago's skyline and lakefront**

**Throughout the years, Chicago has been given all kinds of nicknames.
If you could give Chicago a nickname, what would if be?
Fill in your answer above.**

SWAMPLAND AND SMELLY ONIONS

Long before skyscrapers loomed in Chicago, the Potawatomi Indian tribe settled in what was once a marshy section of land covered with wild onion plants. The name "Chicago" probably comes from the Potawatomi word *che-ca-gou*, meaning "stinking wild onions."

The first European visitors to Chicago were two French explorers, Jacques Marquette and Louis Jolliet, who paddled down the Chicago River in 1673. Years later, in the 1770s, an African American fur trader named Jean Baptiste Point DuSable came to the area from New Orleans. He built a log cabin along the banks of the Chicago River and ran a very successful trading business. DuSable lived here for over 30 years and is considered the founder of Chicago.

⬆ **You're never far from the water in Chicago.**

One of Chicago's finest museums, the DuSable Museum of African American History, is named after Jean Baptiste Point DuSable.

SILLY STORY

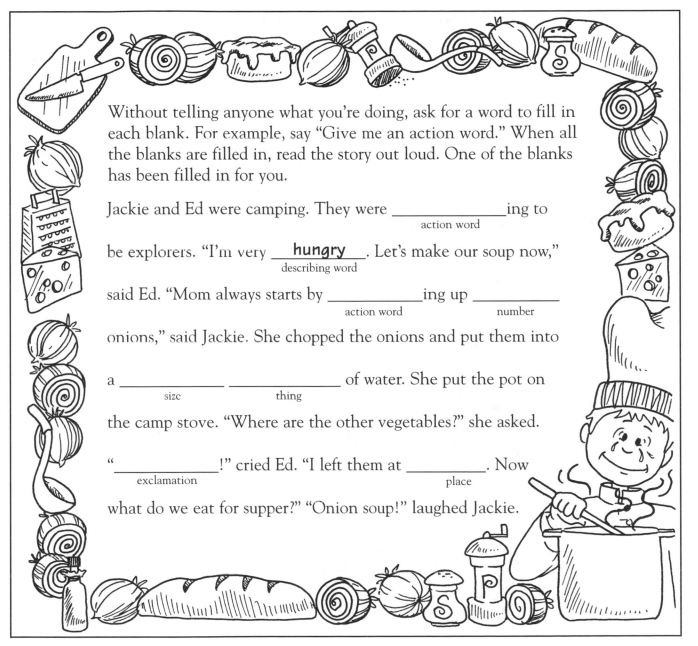

Without telling anyone what you're doing, ask for a word to fill in each blank. For example, say "Give me an action word." When all the blanks are filled in, read the story out loud. One of the blanks has been filled in for you.

Jackie and Ed were camping. They were _____ing to

action word

be explorers. "I'm very ___hungry___. Let's make our soup now,"

describing word

said Ed. "Mom always starts by _____ing up _____

action word   number

onions," said Jackie. She chopped the onions and put them into

a _____ _____ of water. She put the pot on

size   thing

the camp stove. "Where are the other vegetables?" she asked.

"_____!" cried Ed. "I left them at _____. Now

exclamation   place

what do we eat for supper?" "Onion soup!" laughed Jackie.

POPULATION BOOM

Soon settlers from the East started moving to Chicago. Fort Dearborn was built to protect these white settlers from the Potawatomi and other tribes, who wanted to keep the land for themselves. In 1812 the Indians attacked and destroyed Fort Dearborn. Many people were killed in this battle, known as the Fort Dearborn Massacre.

A few years later Fort Dearborn was rebuilt. Gradually, more people came to live in Chicago, many of whom were fur traders. After the opening of the Erie Canal in 1825, things started to pick up in Chicago. When it was incorporated as a village in 1833, it had a population of 350. Just four years later, the population had grown to 4,000! Once shipping canals were built linking the Chicago River with the Mississippi River, the trade business sky-rocketed. Soon hundreds of railroad tracks crossed the city, with trains carrying thousands of immigrants looking for housing and work in this new, growing city.

⇐ **People flocked to Chicago in the 1800s.**

Greater Chicago

A Very Famous Cow

By 1870 there were 300,000 people living in Chicago. More and more buildings were built to house all these people. Most of these buildings and houses were made of wood. All that wood, along with a dry, hot summer in 1871, added up to big trouble for Chicagoans.

According to legend, on October 8, 1871, a cow kicked over a lantern in Mrs. O'Leary's barn. No one knows for sure if this is true, but we do know that the fire that started in the southwest part of town lasted for 27 hours, destroyed 17,000 buildings, and left over 100,000 people homeless.

 **An artist's drawing of Mrs. O'Leary's cow**

But Chicagoans have always been tough. Within a few days businesses reopened. Optimistic architects felt they could rebuild Chicago, and they did. Two years later, Chicago was rebuilt with stones and bricks instead of wood.

Another record-breaking fire, the Peshtigo Fire in Wisconsin, took place on the exact same date as the Great Chicago Fire.

THE 1893 WORLD'S FAIR

In 1893 Chicago hosted the World's Columbian Exposition in Jackson Park to celebrate the 400th anniversary of Christopher Columbus' discovery of America. Many cities wanted to host the fair, but the determined Chicagoans won out. The Museum of Science and Industry and the Art Institute were both built for this huge fair. Chicago's subway system, the "El," was also first introduced.

At this major event, electricity was introduced to Americans. Another highlight of the Columbian Exposition was the unveiling of the first Ferris wheel, created by George W. Ferris. The enormous wheel had 36 wooden cars, which held 60 people in each car. Altogether this huge Ferris wheel was able to hold 2,160 passengers! After the fair the Ferris wheel was taken down, and its metal was used for making bridges.

⬆ **The very first Ferris wheel**

The World's Columbian Exposition lasted six months and attracted over 27 million visitors.

GANGSTAS AND ALL THAT JAZZ

Chicago is probably most famous for its crime-ridden past. In the early 1920s, the government made it illegal to sell alcohol. Famous criminals like Al Capone and Bugsy Moran moved to Chicago to run the illegal liquor business.

Buying and selling liquor was big business, and gangs fought over who would control it. One famous battle was the St. Valentine's Day Massacre of February 14, 1929. Al Capone's hit men, disguised as police officers, killed seven people. Most of the victims were from Bugsy Moran's rival gang. On the *Untouchables Tour*, you can see where this and other infamous events took place.

⬆ **Al Capone in 1931**

But there was more than crime going on during the 1920s. Louis Armstrong, one of best jazz musicians of all time, made his name with what came to be called "Chicago Style" jazz.

In 1927, when Al Capone was only 28, he made $105 million— a world's record.

Rough Times

During the 1930s, in the period called the Great Depression, many businesses closed and people all over the country lost their jobs. The Depression hit Chicago hard. In 1931 nearly 1,400 families were kicked out of their homes because they couldn't pay rent.

When the United States entered World War II in 1941, things improved for Chicagoans. The city spent $1.3 billion on factories to supply materials for the war—

⇑ **During the Depression, people in Chicago and other cities waited in lines for free food.**

Fermi conducted his experiment in the squash courts under the stands at Stagg Field.

more than any other city in the United States. The war lifted Chicago out of the Depression. Factories making airplane engines and tanks provided jobs for people who desperately needed them.

World history was made in Chicago on December 2, 1942, when the Italian scientist Enrico Fermi and his associates set off the first man-made nuclear chain reaction at the University of Chicago. This led to the creation of the atomic bomb and the building of nuclear power plants.

"Da Boss"

Richard J. Daley, one of Chicago's most famous mayors, was often referred to as "da boss." He was elected mayor in 1955, and he stayed in that position for 21 years, the longest term of any Chicago mayor. Among other things, Daley was known for granting special favors to friends, including hiring them to run city services.

During Daley's long reign as mayor, Chicago grew quickly. Architects built more and more skyscrapers. O'Hare, the world's busiest airport, was also built. New expressways plowed through small neighborhoods. Mayor Daley was proud of his large, bustling city and called Chicago "the City That Works."

Since Daley's time other notable mayors have been elected in Chicago, including Mayor Jane Byrne, Chicago's first female mayor, and Harold Washington, Chicago's first African American mayor.

⬆ **Mayor Richard Daley, 1968**

"Richie" Daley, son of "da boss," followed in his father's footsteps and became Chicago's mayor in 1987. He's still mayor today.

THE "MELTING POT"

Today Chicago is home to nearly 3 million people who live on the north, south, and west sides. (Chicago does not have an "east" side—if it did, it would be in Lake Michigan!)

Chicago is made up of many neighborhoods. People of Chinese, Irish, Greek, and Polish descent can be found in clusters throughout the city. Each of these neighborhoods has its own flavor and history. If you were to walk through Chinatown, you would see signs in Chinese. Even the money machines have instructions in Chinese. In Greektown you'd find lots of Greek restaurants and hear people speaking Greek. And Chicago has the highest population of Polish people outside of Warsaw, the capital of Poland!

⬆ **The gate to Chicago's Chinatown**

On St. Patrick's Day, the city dumps vats of green dye into the Chicago River so everyone can have a bit of Irish luck.

FAMOUS FOLK

Chicago may not have as many movie stars as Los Angeles or New York, but it does have its share of celebrities. Stars often visit the Windy City to film movies. Keep your eyes open! Maybe you'll see a film crew on the Chicago streets.

⬆ **Oprah Winfrey**

Oprah Winfrey films her talk show in Chicago and can sometimes be seen jogging along the lake or doing sit-ups at her health club, the East Bank Club. Sports fans might enjoy watching Chicago Cubs star Sammy Sosa hit one out of the park at Wrigley Field. And future writers might like to order a cheeseburger at the Billy Goat's Tavern, where many famous Chicago newspaper reporters eat lunch.

WIND, SLEET, AND SNOW

Most Chicagoans would agree that Chicago's weather is not high on their list of reasons for living in the city. The long, cold winters can be harsh. The northeast wind, affectionately known as "the Hawk," can feel as if it's cutting right through your winter coat. Even Lake Michigan freezes into huge chunks of ice around its edges. So if you do decide to visit Chicago in the winter, bring a tight-fitting hat, a thick scarf, cozy mittens or gloves, and the warmest coat you own—you'll need them.

Spring starts late in Chicago and often feels too short. Before you know it, the hot, lazy days of summer have arrived, and Chicagoans head for the beach, where it's cooler. The lake, though, usually doesn't warm up until August. Fall is wonderful, with lots of brightly colored leaves and moderate temperatures.

Here are some ideas of what to take when you're out exploring Chicago.

camera · backpack · bathing suit · map · windbreaker · sunglasses · sweatshirt · snack · jeans · comfortable walking shoes · cap · water bottle · important numbers and addresses · rain gear · pocket change · Shorts

2 PARKS AND THE GREAT OUTDOORS

CHICAGO HAS BEEN CALLED "CITY OF PARKS" because of its amazing array of parks along the lake. With over 580 parks in the city, there's something for everyone in the family. Tennis courts, golf courses, and winding bike paths are just a few of the activities the Chicago Park District has to offer.

Lake Michigan, too, keeps visitors and natives busy with lots of boating, swimming, and wind-surfing options. If you're visiting in the summer, Chicago has over 20 miles of beaches, where you can sunbathe, body surf, or build sand castles.

⇑ Sand and skyscrapers at Oak Street Beach

Parks and the Great Outdoors

1. **Grant Park/Buckingham Fountain**
2. **Lincoln Park Conservatory**
3. **North Park Village Nature Center**
4. **Oak Street Beach**
5. **Oz Park**
6. **Skate on State**

OAK STREET BEACH

What do you do in Chicago when the temperature soars into the 100s? You do what most Chicagoans do: you go to the beach.

Probably the most popular beach in Chicago is Oak Street Beach. People come from all over the city to hang out at this hot spot, with its clean water and well-kept beach. On any given day you can see joggers, Rollerbladers, and bikers cruising down the cement walkway searching for the perfect people-watching spot. It's a great place to toss a Frisbee or play a game of volleyball.

But what makes Oak Street Beach so unusual is its location. Stretched out in front of you is enormous Lake Michigan. But on the north, south, and west sides of the beach are Chicago's famous skyscrapers.

↑ **You can cool down right near downtown at Oak Street Beach.**

On a very hot day the population of Oak Street Beach can reach 50,000!

WHAT'S THE DIFFERENCE?

These two pictures might look the same, but they are not. See if you can find all the differences between the two scenes. Hint: There are at least 15 differences.

OZ PARK

Frank L. Baum, the author of *The Wizard of Oz*, once lived a few blocks from this park, named after his famous book. Standing guard at the entrance is a statue of the Tin Man. You'll also find some yellow bricks on the northeast corner, as well as a cool play area with castle-like turrets and secret crawl spaces.

If you're lucky, you might catch a game of 16-inch softball being played at this park. Unlike 12-inch softball, which is what most of the country plays, 16-inch softball is played without mitts, and the pitch is high and slow. This form of the game began in Chicago over 100 years ago and is still the most popular type of softball played in the city.

↗ **The Tin Man lives on in Oz Park.**

↑ **The play equipment at Oz Park is lots of fun.**

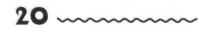

Baum came up with the name Oz from a filing cabinet drawer in his office marked *O-Z*.

CROSSWORD FUN

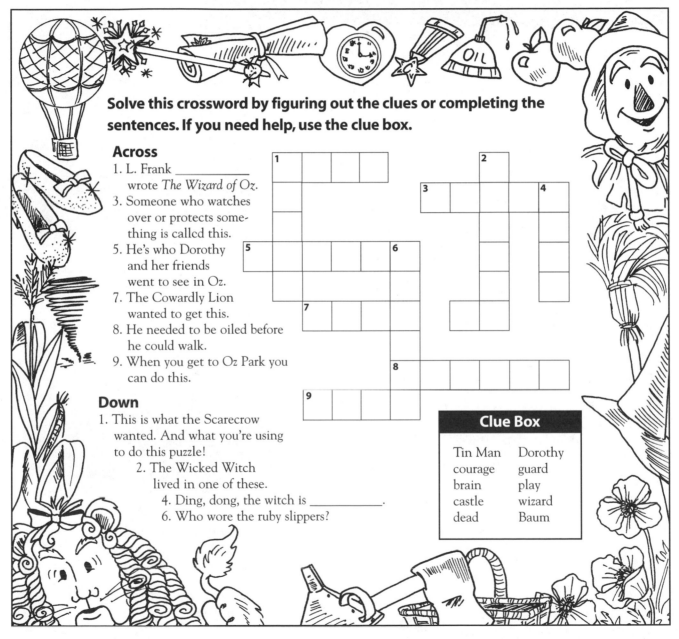

Solve this crossword by figuring out the clues or completing the sentences. If you need help, use the clue box.

Across

1. L. Frank _____ wrote *The Wizard of Oz*.
3. Someone who watches over or protects something is called this.
5. He's who Dorothy and her friends went to see in Oz.
7. The Cowardly Lion wanted to get this.
8. He needed to be oiled before he could walk.
9. When you get to Oz Park you can do this.

Down

1. This is what the Scarecrow wanted. And what you're using to do this puzzle!
2. The Wicked Witch lived in one of these.
4. Ding, dong, the witch is _____.
6. Who wore the ruby slippers?

Clue Box

Tin Man	Dorothy
courage	guard
brain	play
castle	wizard
dead	Baum

GRANT PARK

Grant Park is one of the biggest parks in the city. Free outdoor concerts and **Taste of Chicago**—Chicago's huge outdoor food festival—are held here every year. The park is also home to some of Chicago's greatest museums, including the **Art Institute**, the **Field Museum**, the **Shedd Aquarium**, and the **Adler Planetarium**. The Chicago Bulls have gathered here along with their fans to celebrate all six of their NBA championship victories.

The main attraction in Grant Park is **Buckingham Fountain**, a sight not to be missed on a summer night. The fountain is 280 feet across and shoots water 135 feet into the air! During the summer season colored lights highlight the sprays of water.

Buckingham Fountain sprays water high into the air.

You'll see this statue if you visit Grant Park.

COLOR THE FOUNTAIN

During the summer, Buckingham Fountain is bursting with color.
Color this scene to show all the brightness and beauty
of a summer night in Chicago.

LINCOLN PARK CONSERVATORY

⇧ **Lincoln Park Conservatory**

If the weather is bleak and rainy, step inside this indoor garden for a special treat. Four huge, year-round greenhouses offer a tropical climate, fancy flowers, and exotic plants from faraway places like Brazil, China, and Ethiopia. Lagoons filled with shimmering goldfish will make you want to jump in for a quick dip.

Be sure to visit the 50-foot-tall fiddle-leaf rubber tree, which has been there as long as the conservatory itself. And check out the cactus room, where hundreds of oddly shaped cacti thrive in the dry, sandy atmosphere. You'll also find banana trees, fig trees, and ferns from all over the world.

In the conservatory's Fern House you'll find *cycads.* This species dates back about 135 million years!

A PICNIC AT THE PARK

Hidden in this word search are the names of some trees, plants, and flowers. Search for words vertically, horizontally, and diagonally. Can you find all 10 words? The first word has been found for you.

Word Box		
maple	rose	violet
oak	aspen	ivy
fern	pine	
dandelion	cactus	

```
K O N A T K M E S O P M Y P V
H D H F I V Y S Y M H E B R O
N Y A L S I A I M O P T S O L
T T S N D O S K C A C T U S L
A A P W D L N R D K P E N E E
S E E E M E F N G N N L G T Y
P I N E G T L N H U I U E E B
E A X S P C I I D K C L M R A
N O N D U K R O O B O A N M L
U I S E I S F E R N Y D N L L
R O T B L K I P E U L I M Y N
D Y D N I O P Y F R I S B E H
```

SKATE ON STATE

There's no reason why the cold weather should keep you indoors if you're visiting Chicago in the winter. Grab your skates and head over to Skate on State, one of Chicago's most popular outdoor skating rinks.

Located across from **Marshall Fields**, a famous Chicago department store, this ice rink has it all. If you don't have your own skates, you can rent them at this rink. Or polish up your skating skills on Saturday, when Skate on State offers free skating lessons. If you're not in the mood to skate, you can always watch demonstrations from local skaters as they show off their jumps and spins. Afterwards, glide across the street to Marshall Fields and warm up with a cup of hot chocolate in the **Walnut Room**.

During the off season, Skate on State is known as Gallery 37, where Chicago students display their artwork.

⬆ **Wintertime at Skate on State**

FILL IN THE ICE SKATER

Imagine you're skating at Skate on State. Draw yourself in the blank space above making a fancy move, and then color the scene.

NORTH PARK VILLAGE NATURE CENTER

Who says cities are made of only concrete and tall buildings? The North Park Village Nature Center is a quiet nature retreat on the northwest side of Chicago. The site of a farm in the 1800s, the nature center is now a place where you can hike through four different native habitats—wetlands, woodlands, prairie, and oak savanna. Programs like Prairie Prowls, Star Watches, Turtle Show-and-Tell, and Wetland Walks are offered throughout the year.

Even if you don't attend a special program, there's still plenty to do here. The **Education Center** has hands-on displays about nature and a live animal room, where you just might meet a turtle or two.

Coyotes are now living in the city of Chicago and are quickly adapting to city life.

↥ **A pond at the North Park Village Nature Center**

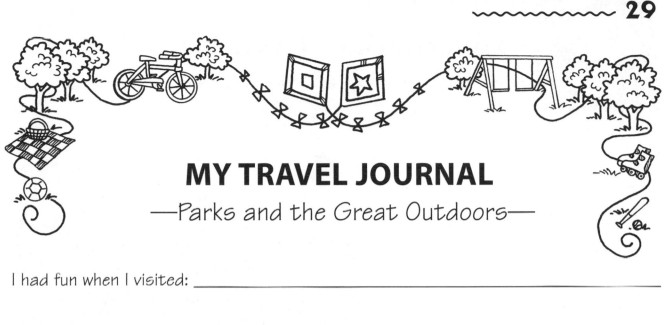

MY TRAVEL JOURNAL
—Parks and the Great Outdoors—

I had fun when I visited: _____

I learned about: _____

My favorite park was: _____

This is a picture of what I saw at a park in Chicago

3 ANIMALS, ANIMALS

ANIMAL LOVERS WILL HAVE PLENTY of critters to coo at in Chicago. For those with exotic tastes, there are koala bears, pythons, penguins, and more at the Lincoln Park Zoo. You can also pet a chinchilla at the Children's Zoo or watch a cow being milked in the zoo's farm. The Indian Boundary Zoo is a much smaller zoo on the west side where you can see deer, goats, and sheep up close. Horse lovers will enjoy watching carriage horses being groomed and fed at the Noble Horse Equestrian Center. And dog lovers everywhere will howl at the antics of neighborhood pooches as they splash in the waves at Doggy Beach.

At the Lincoln Park Zoo you can even feed a cow.

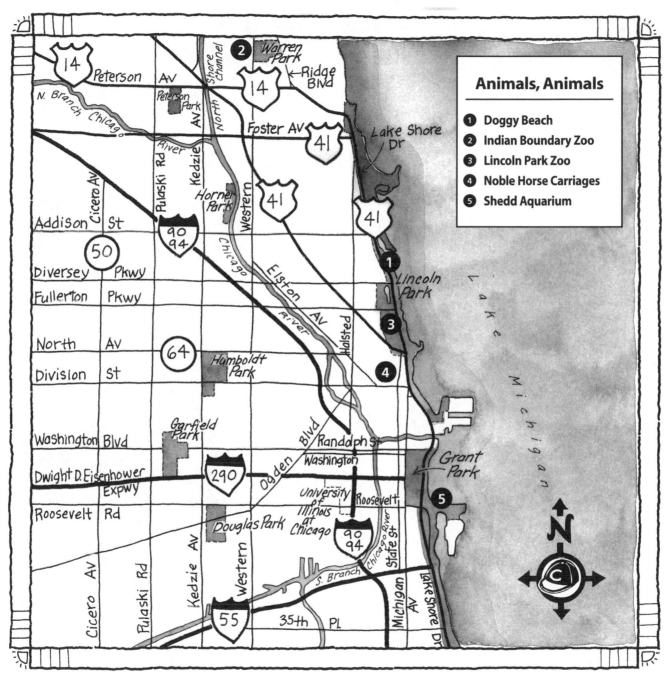

Animals, Animals

1. Doggy Beach
2. Indian Boundary Zoo
3. Lincoln Park Zoo
4. Noble Horse Carriages
5. Shedd Aquarium

LINCOLN PARK ZOO

The oldest zoo in the world and one of the only free zoos left, Lincoln Park Zoo is a great place to start your animal safari in Chicago. With 1,000 animals to visit, you're sure to run into your favorite ones here. On a warm day, stop and watch the seals as they clown around in their huge outdoor pool near the entrance. Or visit the cuddly koalas, who doze most of the day on the tops of the zoo's eucalyptus trees.

Maybe you prefer scaly, slithering critters. If so, you'll love the new **Small Mammals–Reptile House**, where many threatened and endangered species are on display. You'll see the Virgin Islands boa, one of the world's most endangered snakes, and the brush-tailed bettong, a member of the kangaroo family, along with lots of other cold- and warm-blooded creatures.

⇑ **Koala bears are hard to resist.**

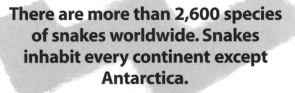

⇑ **You can reach out and touch some of the animals at the zoo.**

There are more than 2,600 species of snakes worldwide. Snakes inhabit every continent except Antarctica.

CONNECT THE DOTS

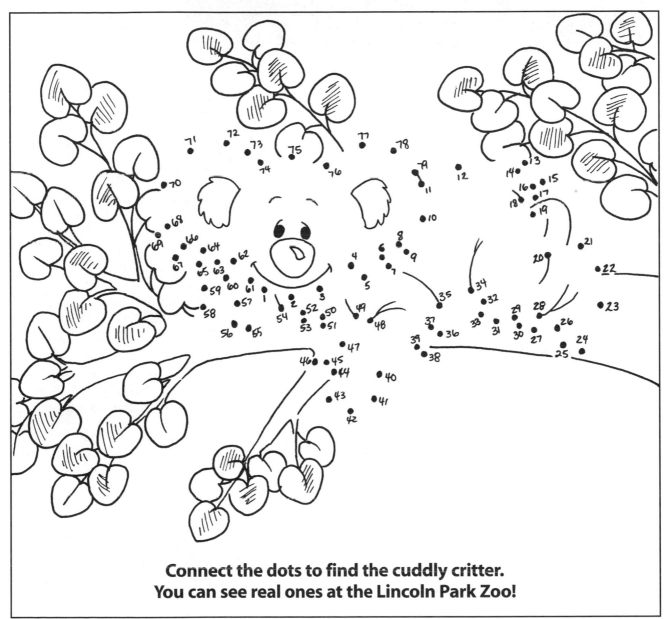

Connect the dots to find the cuddly critter.
You can see real ones at the Lincoln Park Zoo!

THE JOHN G. SHEDD AQUARIUM

The Shedd Aquarium is the largest indoor aquarium in the world. It houses over 6,000 aquatic animals, from huge alligator snapping turtles to tiny seahorses. The galleries surrounding the Coral Reef Tank each have a different focus and include saltwater and freshwater fish.

If you don't have any plans for lunch, drop by the Shedd Aquarium between 11 a.m. and 2 p.m., when divers hand feed sharks, turtles, and tropical fish in the 90,000 gallon Coral Reef Tank. You can hear the diver talk about the fish he's feeding while watching him pet them as they swim by.

For an extra fee, you can visit the new Oceanarium. It re-creates a North Pacific coastline, with nature trails that lead you to beluga whales, otters, and seals, as well as a nearby colony of penguins.

↑ **You can see this beluga whale at the Oceanarium.**

It took 364 tons of salt to make the 3 million gallons of salt water in the Oceanarium.

WHAT'S WRONG HERE?

**Something fishy is going on at the Shedd Aquarium.
See if you can find the ten things wrong with this scene.**

DOGGY BEACH

You won't find many string bikinis at the Doggy Beach, but you will find lots of Frisbees, old tennis balls, and leashes. The only beach in Chicago dedicated to four-legged sun bathers, Doggy Beach is the best place to take Rover on a hot Chicago afternoon. Even if you don't own a dog, stop by and watch all the various mutts, Dobermans, poodles, and dalmatians chase each other, fetch sticks, and swim in the lake. Dog lovers shouldn't miss this fenced-off beach, which attracts dozens of dogs and their owners during the "dog days" of summer.

The American water spaniel has a long, feathery tail that helps him steer in the water.

⇡ **If you like dogs, you'll love this beach.**

DOG GONE CRAZY

**The dogs at Doggy Beach are having a fine old time.
Color in this doggy-delightful scene.**

NOBLE HORSE EQUESTRIAN CENTER

You can recognize an Appaloosa by its spotted rump.

Tucked away in the heart of Old Town is a horse lover's paradise. The Noble Horse Equestrian Center is a livery stable that once housed horses that delivered goods. Today the horses that live here have easier jobs. They give pleasure rides!

The best time to visit the Noble Horse is between 4 and 6 p.m. on weekdays, when groomers feed the horses and polish the carriages as they prepare for their evening rides. You can pet a Morgan, an Appaloosa, or even one of the bigger Belgians. In addition to its carriage service, the Noble Horse Equestrian Center offers riding lessons so you can brush up on your horseback riding skills. Check out the enormous barn and watch expert riders as they gallop around the 200-by-75-foot ring. Giddyap!

⬆ Your carriage awaits at the Noble Horse Equestrian Center.

WHAT'S IN COMMON?

Each of these horses has something in common with the other two in the same row. For example, the horses in the middle row all have hair near their hooves. Draw a line through each row and describe what the horses in that row have in common. Don't forget to include diagonals!

INDIAN BOUNDARY ZOO

Although this tiny zoo doesn't have as many animals as Lincoln Park Zoo, it's still a fun place to visit. You'll find a variety of animals here, mostly hooved ones, like African pygmy goats, white-tailed deers, and alpacas (they look a lot like llamas), but also mute swans. And for the next couple of years the zoo will be developing a special bird, bat, and butterfly exhibit that lovers of flying creatures are sure to enjoy.

Next door to the zoo is the **Indian Boundary Park**, a great place for horsing around. It has ladders, turrets, tunnels, slides, bridges, a haunted mansion, a train, teepees, a tire mountain, and more. During the hot summer months you can cool off at the huge sprinkler, so be sure to wear a bathing suit and bring a towel. Afterwards, you can feed the wild ducks in the duckpond.

You'll see goats and other animals up close at this small zoo.

Alpacas and llamas are both members of the camel family.

MY TRAVEL JOURNAL

—Animals, Animals—

I had fun when I visited: _____

I learned about: _____

_____

My favorite animal was: _____

This is a picture of an animal I saw

4 LANDMARKS, SKYSCRAPERS, AND THE ARTS

CHICAGO IS THE BIRTHPLACE OF THE modern building. In 1885 the world's first skyscraper, the nine-story Home Insurance Building, was built in Chicago. Since that time Chicago has been known for its bold, creative architecture, especially its skyscrapers.

Just as interesting as the world-famous architecture in Chicago are the outdoor sculptures. Famous artists, including Pablo Picasso, Joan Miro, and Marc Chagall, created monumental sculptures for Chicago's outdoor sculpture gallery. Many of the sculptures are abstract designs that have become popular over the years. There are over 97 sculptures in downtown Chicago, with nicknames like "Plug Bug," the "Batcolumn" (which looks like a huge baseball bat), and "Big Beaver."

⇡ **Abstract sculptures have fanciful designs.**

Landmarks, Skyscrapers and the Arts

1. **Chicago Cultural Center**
2. **Harold Washington Library**
3. **John Hancock**
4. **Rosehill Cemetery**
5. **Sears Tower**
6. **State of Illinois Center (Thompson Center)**
7. **Untitled Picasso sculpture**
8. **Water Tower Pumping Building/Water Tower**

THE SEARS TOWER

A visit to Chicago would not be complete without the 55-second-long elevator ride up to the observation deck of the Sears Tower. Your ears will probably pop a dozen times, but it will all be worth it once you gaze out from the 103rd floor. On a clear day, you should be able to see Michigan, Indiana, and Wisconsin.

Can you guess how many windows this 110-story building has? If you said 16,000, you guessed right. No, they don't ask window washers to soar up 1,450 feet to clean the windows! Six automatic window washing machines complete the task eight times a year. This sleek steel and glass building was built in 1973 and cost over $150 million to construct.

⇡ **The Sears Tower really does scrape the sky.**

Wall climber "Spider" Dan Goodwin successfully scaled both the Sears Tower and the John Hancock in the 1980s.

WHAT'S WRONG HERE?

In this Chicago scene there are some pretty strange things going on.
Try to find at least 12 things wrong with this scene.

THE JOHN HANCOCK CENTER

Another gigantic skyscraper in Chicago is the John Hancock Center. With 100 stories, it is Chicago's second tallest building. At 1,107 feet high, "Big John" is 343 feet shorter than the Sears Tower. It still took 11,459 panes of glass and 46,000 tons of steel to make this impressive building. The crisscross beams on the front help keep it from swaying in the powerful Lake Michigan wind.

Many people like visiting the John Hancock Center's newly remodeled observatory on the 94th floor because the views of Lake Michigan are so spectacular. On a clear summer day, you can see 80 miles in all directions. If the wind is right, you might also see hundreds of boats sailing on the lake. Be sure to check out the screened-in open skyway, where you can see, feel, hear, and even smell downtown Chicago. And don't miss Windows on Chicago, which uses virtual technology to show you the city's most popular sites.

⇑ **The John Hancock Tower (right) is another giant on the Chicago skyline.**

MATCH THE SAILBOATS

Each of these sailboats has an exact match. Draw a line connecting each of the pairs.

PICASSO'S "UNTITLED" SCULPTURE

Is it a cow? Is it a woman? Or is it a baboon? Picasso's untitled sculpture in front of the **Daley Center** keeps Chicagoans guessing. When it was first unveiled in 1967, "the Picasso," as it is known to most, caused quite a ruckus. Some felt it was too big. Others didn't like its abstract design. Today most Chicagoans are proud of this work of art and regard it as a symbol of Chicago.

The first large-scale abstract sculpture to appear in Chicago, "the Picasso" stretches 50 feet into the air. Picasso used Cor-Ten steel, an industrial steel normally used for buildings, to make this sculpture. Over the years it has changed colors, from gray to a warm, deep brown.

⬆
Chicago loves its Picasso.

Pablo Picasso is considered by many to be the most influential artist of the 1900s. His career spanned over 70 years.

NAME THAT SCULPTURE

**Look at the above abstract sculptures and decide what you think they are.
You can come up with more than one idea for each—
there are no right answers for this activity!**

> The Water Tower was once described as looking like a sand castle that you might find at the bottom of a fish bowl.

THE WATER TOWER

The Chicago Fire destroyed over 17,000 buildings—almost every building in the city. Probably because it was built with limestone instead of wood, the Water Tower was one of two buildings in the area left standing, along with the **Chicago Avenue Pumping Station** across the street. Today the Water Tower houses City Gallery, which features art by local artists.

Across from the Water Tower is the Chicago Avenue Pumping Station, which still serves the city's demand for fresh water. The Pumping Station pumps 250 million gallons of water a day, supplying water to about 390,000 Chicagoans. It's also a tourist information center. You can find out about special events, festivals, current museum exhibits, parades, and performances in Chicago.

←‥

Stop by the Water Tower before you begin your Chicago tour.

WORD SEARCH

Hidden in this word search are the names of some Chicago-related people and things. Search for words vertically, horizontally, and diagonally. Can you find all 10 words? The first word has been found for you.

Word Box

Capone	jazz	Bears
Sears	dinosaurs	Jordan
onions	Oprah	
lake	wind	

```
K O N A T K M E S O P M Y P D
H P H O N I O N S M H B B A I
N Y N L S G A R N O P E S B N
T T P C D R V K A T P A G U O
R A B A G A N L J V C R N T S
D E U P S D F N A N N S A T A
J D S O G A N N Z K I U Y H U
O A N N P C I N Z K E L M R R
R I S E A R S P W W O A N F S
D I S E I S U R N P I D N I L
A O T B L K I V E U L N M Y N
N Y D N I O P Y F R I S D E E
```

HAROLD WASHINGTON LIBRARY

Book lovers will go crazy over this enormous library with its 2 million books and 70 miles of shelving. Named after Chicago's first African American mayor, the Harold Washington Library is the largest lending library in the world. You'll find over 100,000 books in the children's library alone!

↑ **The Washington Library is quite a sight.**

But books aren't the only attraction in this library. The Thomas Hughes Children's Library always has something going on, whether it's a puppet show, story time event, craft lesson, or special performance. You can also explore NatureConnections, a natural history collection, and the Learning Center, a computer center.

Be sure to visit the top floor Winter Garden while you're there. With a glass dome 52 feet above your head and five tall trees around you, it's a great spot to read a book.

HIDE AND SEEK

**There are some unusual things hidden in this library scene.
See if you can find them: apple, flower, dinosaur, football,
frog, hamburger, roller-skate, steering wheel, toothbrush, worm.**

THE ROSEHILL CEMETERY

For something a little different, why not explore Rosehill Cemetery? You'll definitely find lots of interesting monuments, as well as five small lakes filled with geese.

For starters, check out the Volunteer Fireman's Monument. It's marked by a statue of a volunteer fireman holding a coiled hose and a megaphone. Or look for a large granite train entering a tunnel—that's the grave of George Bang, who was head of the Railway Mail Service.

Civil War buffs take note: over 200 Union soldiers are buried here, as well as Civil War generals and heroes.

The Infantryman honors Union soldiers killed during the Civil War.

The Rosehill Cemetery was established by Chicago's first mayor, William Ogden, in 1859.

GUESS WHO THEY WERE

Each of these gravestones shows something about the person who is buried there. See if you can tell by the grave what each person used to do.

CHICAGO CULTURAL CENTER

The Chicago Cultural Center has been wowing visitors since it was first built in 1897. First used as Chicago's public library, this grand building is lavishly decorated with rare marble, intricate mosaics, and a breathtaking stained-glass dome. It's now used for the Chicago Office of Tourism Visitor Center. Stop by and ask about Chicago's upcoming events and special programs and pick up some free brochures. While you're there, take a tour of the building. Whether it's a free art class or a dance performance, there's always something exciting going on at the Chicago Cultural Center.

On the first floor of the building you'll find the **Museum of Broadcast Communications**, where you can anchor your own newscast. Or watch the "One Minute Miracle," featuring award-winning television commercials from around the world.

⇡ **Would you like to anchor your own newscast?**

The Museum of Broadcast Communication's archives contain 12,000 television programs and 50,000 hours of radio programs for you to enjoy.

SILLY STORY

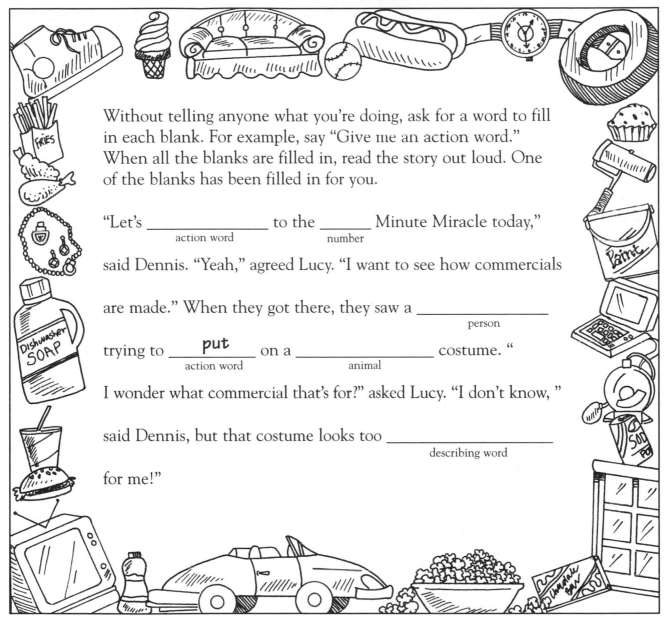

Without telling anyone what you're doing, ask for a word to fill in each blank. For example, say "Give me an action word." When all the blanks are filled in, read the story out loud. One of the blanks has been filled in for you.

"Let's _____ to the _____ Minute Miracle today,"
action word number

said Dennis. "Yeah," agreed Lucy. "I want to see how commercials

are made." When they got there, they saw a _____
person

trying to __**put**_____ on a _____ costume. "
action word animal

I wonder what commercial that's for?" asked Lucy. "I don't know, "

said Dennis, but that costume looks too _____
describing word

for me!"

Outside the James R. Thompson Center is one of Chicago's most famous outdoor sculptures, _Monument with Standing Beast_, by Jean Dubuffet.

THE THOMPSON CENTER

The best things about this building are the glass elevators that whisk visitors up and down 16 floors. You'll love watching the floor of the building get smaller and smaller as you cruise to the top. This bright and airy building has over 24,600 windows!

After you've flown up and down the elevators for awhile, check out the indoor waterfall and have a snack at the food court. Then stroll through an art gallery, shop for some souvenirs, or have your shoes repaired. People can even pay their electricty bills or buy a fishing license here.

But the _coolest_ thing about the Thompson Center is its ice: every night 400 tons of ice are shaped into eight huge cubes. During the day, these mega–ice cubes cool the air distributed throughout the building.

⟵ **It's a long way down on the glass elevators.**

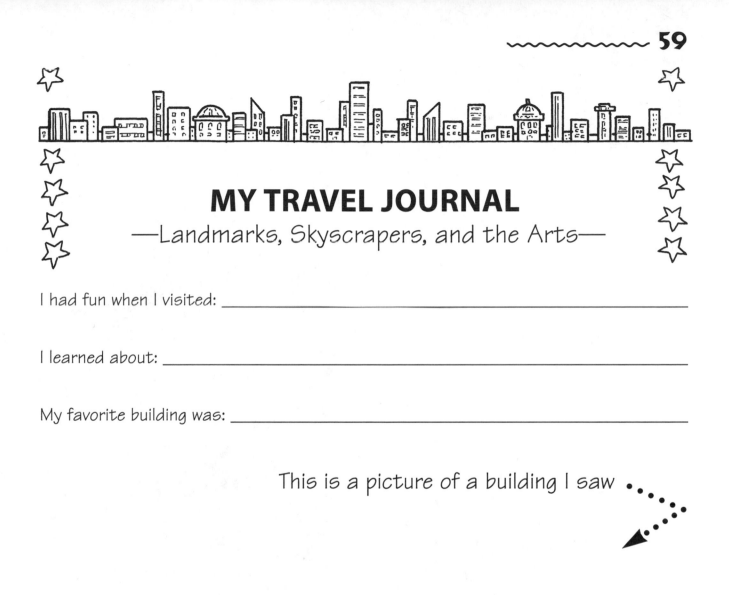

MY TRAVEL JOURNAL
—Landmarks, Skyscrapers, and the Arts—

I had fun when I visited: _____

I learned about: _____

My favorite building was: _____

This is a picture of a building I saw

5 GOOD SPORTS

IT'S PROBABLY A GOOD IDEA TO BONE UP ON your sports trivia before you arrive in Chicago, since sports tend to be the topic of conversation wherever you go. Whether they're complaining about the Cubs or raving about coaches, Chicago fans are *crazy* about their sports. Bulls jackets and Sox hats are practically the city's uniforms. And everybody, yes *everybody*, loves Sammy Sosa.

So get ready to argue about teams, players, and owners. It's a city-wide pastime. Buy your Cubs tickets in advance and sing "Take Me Out to the Ballgame" during the seventh inning stretch. And never, ever say anything nice about the New York Knicks.

⇧ **The Chicago Bulls and the Dallas Mavericks square off.**

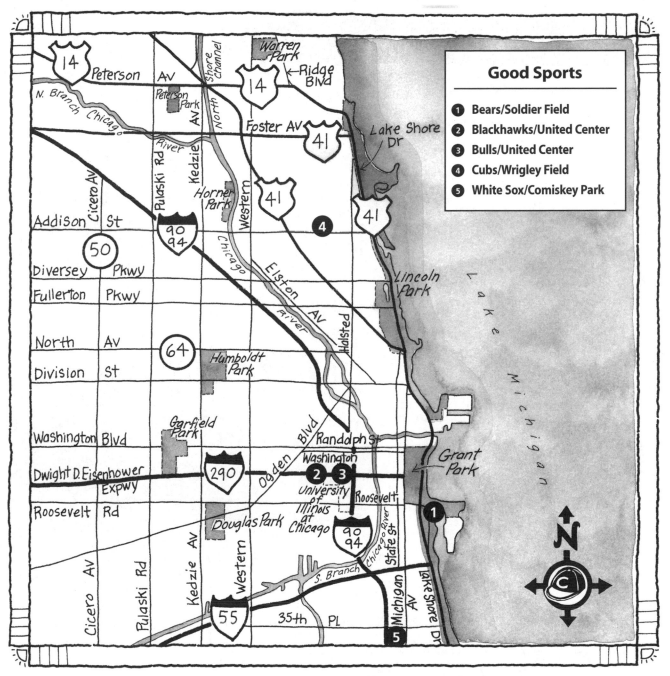

Good Sports

1. Bears/Soldier Field
2. Blackhawks/United Center
3. Bulls/United Center
4. Cubs/Wrigley Field
5. White Sox/Comiskey Park

THE CUBS

Everyone loves to joke about the Cubs baseball team. After all, they haven't been in the World Series since 1945. As the joke goes, *Cubs* stands for *Can't you beat somebody?* Some believe the team hasn't won because of the curse that was placed on it years ago. Way back in 1945, the owner of the famous Billy Goat Tavern, Sam Sianis, tried attending a game with his goat and was told to leave. The angry Sianis put a curse on the team, claiming the Cubs would not win another World Series until his goat was allowed in the ballpark.

Despite the Cubs' long-standing losing streak, fans still pack the ballpark each season. The ivy-covered walls and real grass make **Wrigley Field** one of the finest places in the country to watch a ballgame on a sunny day. It's also where Babe Ruth made sports history when he pointed to the bleachers and then hit a home run there.

Ernie Banks, otherwise known as "Mr. Cub," hit his 500th home run on May 12, 1970, in Wrigley Field.

⬆ **When the Cubs are at home, they play at Wrigley Field.**

COLOR THE BILLY GOAT

**Looks like they finally let Sam Sianis' billy goat into Wrigley Field!
Color this *baaahty* scene.**

THE BULLS

The day that Michael Jordan announced he was retiring from basketball was a very sad one for people in Chicago. His outstanding athletic ability made him a superstar with a capital "S."

Just how good was Michael Jordan? Well, let's see. He won ten National Basketball Association (NBA) scoring titles, more than anyone else. He received the NBA Finals Most Valuable Player award in 1991, 1992, 1993, 1996, 1997, and 1998. He was the only player ever to receive it six times. And while he was playing for the Bulls he sometimes scored up to 50 points per game. Whew!

The Bulls have not had as much success since Michael Jordan left. But they have lots of promising new players and the Chicago fans still love to watch them play!

The Bulls play at the United Center. Outside the stadium is a life-size bronze statue of Michael Jordan.

Bull Toni Kukoc battles for the ball. ⇒

CONNECT THE DOTS

Will one of these boys grow up to become a basketball star? Connect the dots and color this picture.

THE BEARS

"The Monsters of the Midway," as the Bears football team is known, have had some colorful players over the years, as well as some colorful coaches. George Halas—"Papa Bear"— coached the tough Bears for 40 years and was also the owner. He was the only man elected to the Football Hall of Fame in three categories, as player, coach, and owner. He also founded the National Football League (NFL). His team held the record for winning the most games until Don Shula's Miami Dolphins broke it in 1993.

More recently, Mike Ditka coached the Bears and led them to NFL victory in 1986. Known for his short temper and his constant gum chewing, this former player expected 100 percent from his team.

And what about the players? Gale Sayers, Dick Butkus, Walter "Sweetness" Payton, Mike Singletary, and Jim McMahon are just a few of the famous athletes who've played with the Bears.

⇧ Soldier Field is home to "da Bears."

The Bears won the most one-sided game in history when they beat the Redskins in 1940, 73 to 0.

TRICKY TOUCHDOWN

Help this football player through the maze of opposing tacklers to score a touchdown.

THE BLACKHAWKS

The Blackhawks play ice hockey in the same stadium where the Bulls play basketball, the new **United Center**. When the Blackhawks first played in the United Center in 1995, they filled the stadium—all 20,500 seats! They beat the Oilers in this historic game 5 to 1.

Bobby Hull was perhaps the most famous Blackhawk player ever to hit the ice. He made National Hockey League (NHL) history as the first player to score more than 50 goals in a season. He got the nickname "the Golden Jet" for his golden hair and his super-fast slapshot. He and his son Brett have both won the NHL's Most Valuable Player Award.

⬆ **Get in on the action at the United Center.**

The Blackhawks and other NHL teams use up to 40 pucks per game. Some teams have been known to use 5,000 pucks in one season!

⬅ **Kids can sometimes practice with the Blackhawks.**

WHICH TWO ARE THE SAME?

**These hockey players have a lot in common, but only two
are exactly the same. See if you can find the matching players.**

WHITE SOX

Through the years the White Sox have had a reputation as a great baseball team. One incident, though, almost ruined them for good. In the early days of baseball, players didn't earn much money. So in 1919 gamblers made a deal with the White Sox. If they lost the game on purpose, they'd earn some extra money. Unfortunately, the White Sox went along with this dishonest plan. But when the Sox lost to the Cincinnati Reds, people became suspicious. The Sox had been a sure bet.

A year later the grand jury investigated. The pitcher, Eddie Cicotte, confessed to losing the game deliberately. The whole team was banned from baseball for life. To this day, the players from that 1919 team are known as the "Black Sox."

⬆ **The White Sox play at Comiskey Park.**

Comiskey Park's Behind-the-Scenes summer tour lets you see what the dugout, press box, and locker rooms are really like.

MY TRAVEL JOURNAL
—Good Sports—

I had fun when I visited: _____

My favorite sport is: _____

I like it because: _____

This is a picture of something I saw

6 MUSEUMS AND MORE

CHICAGO MUSEUMS ARE ANYTHING but stuffy. At the Field Museum, you can gaze at the infamous Tsavo lions, who devoured 140 bridge builders. An underground train ride in the Museum of Science and Industry will take you into the dark depths of a coal mine, complete with caves, tunnels, and an explosion! The gift shop at the Mexican Fine Arts Center has an assortment of skull sculptures made of sugar and others made of clay. At the Adler Planetarium you can examine a real moon rock and peer through telescopes. Or go on a dinosaur dig at *Dinosaur Expedition* at the Chicago Children's Museum.

⇑ **A brachiosaurus—or all that's left of it—at Stanley Field Hall**

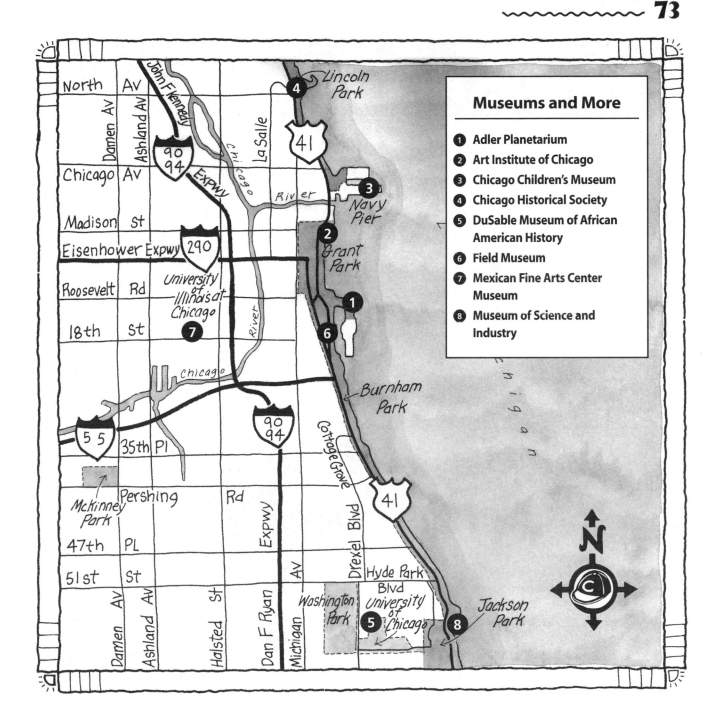

Museums and More

1. **Adler Planetarium**
2. **Art Institute of Chicago**
3. **Chicago Children's Museum**
4. **Chicago Historical Society**
5. **DuSable Museum of African American History**
6. **Field Museum**
7. **Mexican Fine Arts Center Museum**
8. **Museum of Science and Industry**

CHICAGO CHILDREN'S MUSEUM

You won't know where to begin at this museum. As soon as you walk in the door you'll see the three-story *Kovler Family Schooner*. It's a real boat with a crow's nest and a deck perfect for climbing. Slip into a raincoat and pump water 50 feet into the air at *Waterways*, where you can also help build a dam or a fountain. From there, go back 100 million years in *Dinosaur Expedition*, a cool recreation of the Sahara where you can uncover fossils. Or make your own art masterpiece in *Craft Artbounds Studio and Gallery*, an art studio complete with all kinds of clay, paper, and paints.

Explore a log cabin or climb into a tree house at *Treehouse Trails*. Then learn about some of the ways people have coped with prejudice in *Face to Face, Dealing with Prejudice and Discrimination*. In the *Safe and Sound* exhibit, you can sit in a realistic ambulance with flashing lights or look at real x-rays.

You'll see dinosaur bones and lots of other neat things at the Chicago Children's Museum. ⇨

WHAT'S THE DIFFERENCE?

**These two scenes with schooners might look the same, but they are not.
Can you find all the differences between the two pictures?
Hint: There are at least 12 differences.**

THE FIELD MUSEUM

Imagine standing in front of a four-story brachiosaurus, two fighting African bull elephants and huge Northwest Coast Indian totem poles. These are just a few of the things that will greet you when you walk through the doors of the Field Museum, one of the world's best museums for exploring dinosaurs, mummies, and ancient civilizations.

⇑ You won't forget Bushman!

If dinosaurs aren't your thing, perhaps you'd like to see Bushman, the famous Lincoln Park Zoo gorilla, who grew to be 6 feet, 2 inches tall and weighed 575 pounds when he was alive. Or maybe ferocious lions are more your style. The museum has stuffed Tsavo lions, the very same ones that ate 140 East African workers back in 1898.

⇐ **These African elephants are awesome.**

The albertosaurus was able to run down its victims by cruising up to 40 miles per hour.

COLOR TO FIND THE BRACHIOSAURUS

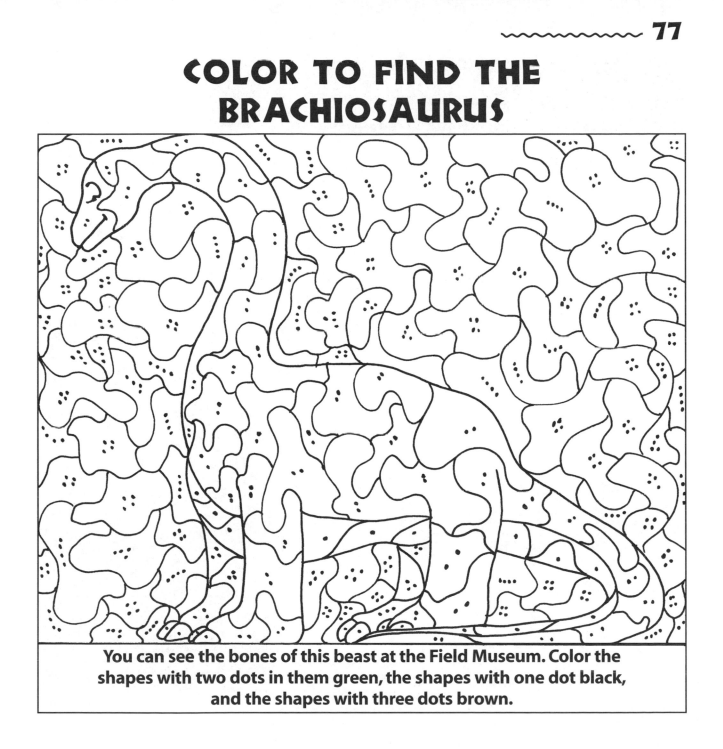

**You can see the bones of this beast at the Field Museum. Color the
shapes with two dots in them green, the shapes with one dot black,
and the shapes with three dots brown.**

THE MUSEUM OF SCIENCE AND INDUSTRY

Ever tried walking through a heart? Probably not. But at this museum you can learn all about this blood-pumping organ while traveling through a 16-foot-high model of it. If you'd rather learn about your brain, there are plenty of smart activities to keep your mind occupied in *The Brain*.

The *Railway Gallery* is a popular exhibit, with a 3,000-square-foot model Santa Fe railroad layout complete with Native American pueblos. In another exhibit you can climb aboard an actual U-505 submarine and watch a movie about how it was once captured. On a smaller scale, you might enjoy visiting the *Fairy Castle*, a dollhouse filled with scenes from famous fairy tales.

Not to be missed is the Omnimax Theater, with its 72-speaker sound system and 5-story curved screen that surrounds you with larger-than-life images.

The Museum of Science and Industry has over 2,000 exhibits!

The Heart is another exhibit that ⇢ takes you right inside the body.

WHAT'S WRONG HERE?

These trains just left their stations. By tracing their tracks, can you tell which station each train started from? Draw lines from the trains to the correct stations.

THE ADLER PLANETARIUM

If stars, planets and constellations make your spine tingle, you'll love the Adler. This museum and planetarium has three floors of exhibits about space exploration, telescopes, the solar system, and astronomy.

Visit the *Early Tools of Astronomy: Universe in Your Hands* exhibit. You'll learn how people have used tools like sundials and telescopes through the ages. In *Gateway to the Universe* you can see how astronomers gather information by studying light from the stars.

On the first floor, check out model rockets, a moon rock, and a meteorite. Or step inside a transporter and "beam up" to a new planet. The new **Sky Pavilion** is a glass area that wraps around the outside of the planetarium. In it you'll find exciting new exhibits about our solar system, the Milky Way.

The Hale-Bopp comet is farther out in space than any other comet discovered so far.

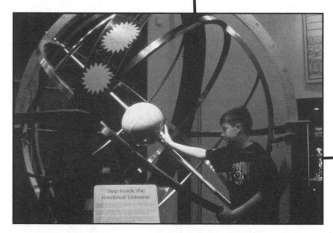

Examine the Earth's rotation at the Adler Planetarium.

WORD SEARCH

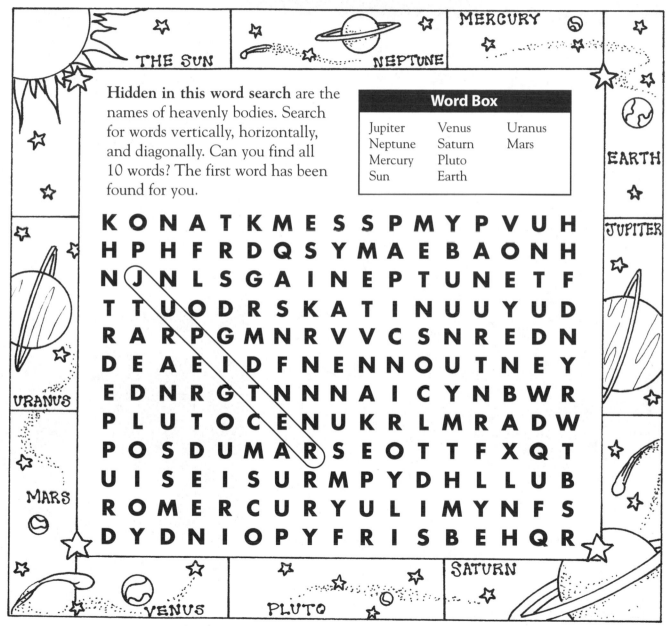

THE SUN
NEPTUNE
MERCURY
EARTH
JUPITER
URANUS
MARS
VENUS
PLUTO
SATURN

Hidden in this word search are the names of heavenly bodies. Search for words vertically, horizontally, and diagonally. Can you find all 10 words? The first word has been found for you.

Word Box		
Jupiter	Venus	Uranus
Neptune	Saturn	Mars
Mercury	Pluto	
Sun	Earth	

K O N A T K M E S S P M Y P V U H
H P H F R D Q S Y M A E B A O N H
N J N L S G A I N E P T U N E T F
T T U O D R S K A T I N U U Y U D
R A R P G M N R V V C S N R E D N
D E A E I D F N E N N O U T N E Y
E D N R G T N N N A I C Y N B W R
P L U T O C E N U K R L M R A D W
P O S D U M A R S E O T T F X Q T
U I S E I S U R M P Y D H L L U B
R O M E R C U R Y U L I M Y N F S
D Y D N I O P Y F R I S B E H Q R

THE ART INSTITUTE

Standing guard at the entrance to the Art Institute of Chicago are two 10-foot-tall bronze lions protecting some of the world's most famous paintings, by artists such as Monet, Renoir, Picasso, and Chagall.

On the lower level of the museum is a great treat for kids—the Thorne Miniature Rooms, 68 dollhouse-like rooms decorated with tiny furniture and lifelike details such as books, knitting needles, and toys. The *California Hallway* even has original miniature paintings by well-known artists like Fernand Leger. As you look through the windows of these rooms you'll see landscapes complete with trees and mountains.

Don't miss Gunsalus Hall, either, which showcases medieval suits of armor, swords, spears, daggers, and horse equipment. The *Arthur Rubloff Paperweight* is another great exhibit, with a dazzling display of glass paperweights from around the world.

The famous bronze lions at the front of the museum have been known to sport Bears helmets, Christmas wreaths, and party hats, depending on the time of year.

⇡ When you see the lions out front, you'll know you're at the Art Institute.

DESIGN A DOLLHOUSE

The rooms in this dollhouse have been left unfinished. Put patterns on the fabrics, fill in the picture frames, add things to the table tops, and then color the scene however you'd like your dollhouse to look.

THE CHICAGO HISTORICAL SOCIETY

Founded in 1856, the Chicago Historical Society is the city's oldest museum. As you walk in, you'll see logs from Fort Dearborn along one wall. In the Illinois Pioneer Life Gallery you can watch demonstrations of flax spinning, weaving, candle dipping, quilting, and other crafts. Why not climb aboard Chicago's first locomotive, The Pioneer? Or watch a movie about the Great Chicago Fire of 1871.

The second floor houses *We the People: Creating a Nation, 1760-1820*, along with *A House Divided: America in the Age of Lincoln*. Here you can see first printings of the Declaration of Independence, the Constitution, and an original copy of the Thirteenth Amendment abolishing slavery, signed by Lincoln.

Another favorite exhibit is *Hands-on History*, where you can re-create the sound effects from a 1930s radio show, touch toys that melted in the Chicago Fire, or step into an early fur trader's cabin.

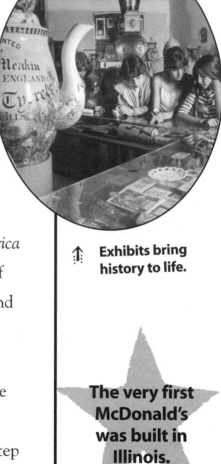

⇡ **Exhibits bring history to life.**

The very first McDonald's was built in Illinois.

CROSSWORD FUN

Solve this crossword by figuring out the clues or completing the sentences. If you need help, use the clue box.

Across

5. Early settlers were called this. It's also the name of Chicago's first locomotive.
6. People built these for protection. Kids like to build them to play in.
7. At the museum you can watch a _____ about the Great Chicago Fire.
8. You wear this to help keep track of time.

Down

1. The city you're visiting.
2. Another word for persons.
3. Quilting, candle-making, and weaving are _____ you can see at the Pioneer Life Gallery.
4. The Chicago _____ Society is the city's oldest museum.
9. The side of a room or a house is called this.

Clue Box

crafts	Chicago	fort
pioneer	people	wall
movie	watch	historical

THE MEXICAN FINE ARTS CENTER

The Mexican Fine Arts Center is the largest Latino cultural institute in the country. In addition to fine exhibits, this museum also offers workshops, theater, and music events focusing on Mexican art and culture.

This museum is probably most famous for its annual *Día de los Muertos*, or Day of the Dead, exhibit. The Day of the Dead is a Mexican celebration in which families remember and honor those who have died. Many families build altars in their homes and prepare food and fresh flowers to tempt departed family members. Some families have picnics in the cemetery as well.

The Mexican Fine Arts Center also has its own radio station where people between the ages of 17 and 25 are trained in all the different aspects of radio production, with an emphasis on Mexican culture.

The Mexican Fine Arts Center has developed a Youth Museum called *Yollocalli*, an ancient Aztec word meaning "home of the heart."

⇑ Express yourself at the Mexican Fine Arts Center.

MATCH THE SOMBREROS

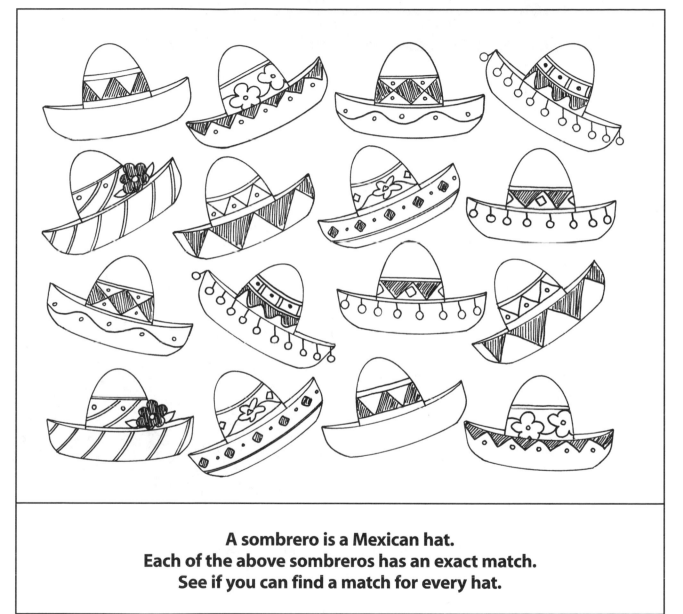

A sombrero is a Mexican hat.
Each of the above sombreros has an exact match.
See if you can find a match for every hat.

THE DuSABLE MUSEUM OF AFRICAN AMERICAN HISTORY

Named after Chicago's first settler, African American Jean Baptiste Pointe DuSable, the DuSable Museum contains over 10,000 paintings, sculptures, prints, and other items related to African American history. In the *Slave Gallery*, with its shackles and scrub boards, you'll see how slaves once lived. Another highlight of the DuSable Museum is a pair of Joe Louis' boxing gloves.

The DuSable Museum also hosts many exciting annual events. Visit at the end of December or in early January and participate in their *Kwanzaa* (African American harvest celebration) workshops. Throughout February they have special programs for Black History Month. During the summer months you and your family will enjoy the Children's Penny Film Series, with fun movies about African folktales.

⇧ Important exhibits teach about the struggle for African American freedom.

Don't forget to visit the gift shop, with dozens of books, games, and jewelry, housed in a replica of Jean Baptiste's log cabin.

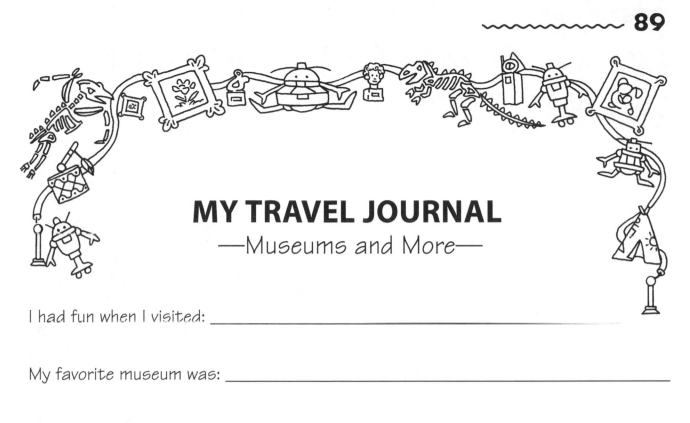

MY TRAVEL JOURNAL
—Museums and More—

I had fun when I visited: _____

My favorite museum was: _____

I learned about: _____

This is a picture of a painting or sculpture I saw

CHICAGO'S A BIG CITY WITH PLENTY OF entertainment possibilities. Whether you want to practice your batting, play a round of miniature golf, or go roller skating, Chicago has it all. Stroll along Navy Pier and you're sure to find some excitement, from a 15-story Ferris wheel to an indoor garden complete with palm trees. Novelty Golf has not one but two miniature golf courses that will challenge even the most seasoned players. As if all that's not enough, the Hidden Peak will test your athletic abilities with its towering rock wall. It's all here in Chicago, waiting for you to give it a try!

If you love basketball, Nike Town is your place.

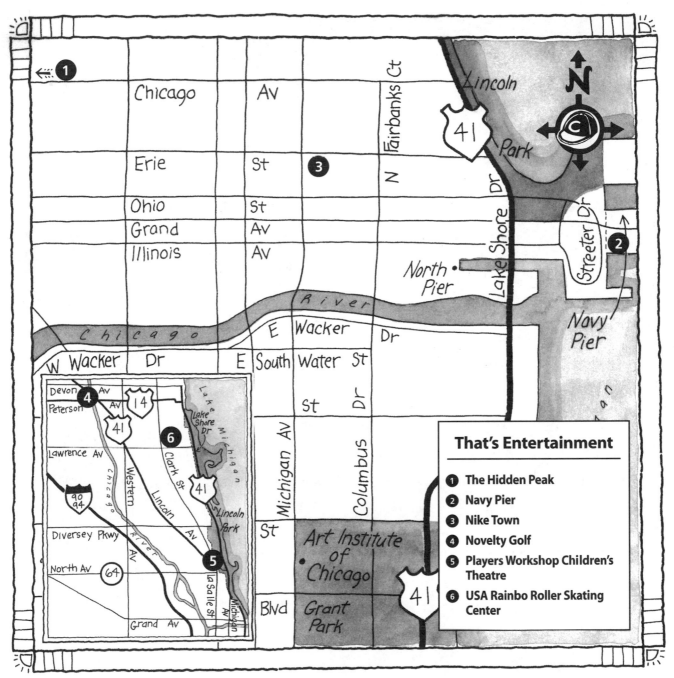

That's Entertainment

1. **The Hidden Peak**
2. **Navy Pier**
3. **Nike Town**
4. **Novelty Golf**
5. **Players Workshop Children's Theatre**
6. **USA Rainbo Roller Skating Center**

NAVY PIER

Navy Pier has a long and interesting history. It was originally designed as a ship terminal. When it first opened, a streetcar line ran out to its tip, which juts 3,040 feet into the water. During World War II it served as a training school for marines. The University of Illinois also had its campus here until 1965.

Navy Pier is now a hotspot for entertainment. It houses the **Chicago Children's Museum**, for one thing, as well as the indoor **Crystal Gardens**, the country's largest glass-enclosed park. If you're in the mood for a little excitement, you can ride the 15-story Ferris wheel or go for a whirl on the carousel, with its 36 custom-built horses. You can also rent a bike or in-line skates.

↑ **Navy Pier is a recreation hot spot.**

On July 4, 1995, Ursula Wonn and John Elrod got married on the top of the 148-foot-high Ferris wheel.

COLOR THE CAROUSEL

Use your favorite colors to fill in this merry-go-round.

USA RAINBO ROLLER SKATING CENTER

You can rent or bring your own roller skates or in-line blades to one of the world's largest roller skating rinks. The Rainbo features two rinks, one for beginners and one for more advanced skaters, so whatever your level, you'll have fun. Zip around the rink to songs played by professional deejays, and hang out in the arcade room when your feet get tired. During the winter they have Wednesday Madness Nights, when you can get in free with a pencil or a bandaid!

The **Rainbo Building** is a Chicago landmark. In the 1930s, it housed jai alai courts, wrestling matches, and dog shows. In the 1950s it was known as the Million Dollar Ballroom, a place where people could go to hear big bands. It was called the Electric Theater in the 1960s and featured bands like the Rolling Stones. In 1979 it was sold to the United Skates of America and has been mobbed by diehard roller skaters ever since.

Roll on into the Rainbo Roller Skating Center.

WHAT'S IN COMMON?

Each of these skaters has something in common with the other two in the same row. For example, the skaters in the middle row all have wrist protectors on. Draw a line through each row and describe what the horses in that row have in common. Don't forget to include diagonals!

NOVELTY GOLF

If you think you might be the next Tiger Woods, try your hand at the most challenging miniature golf course in all of Chicago—Novelty Golf. This 50-year-old course has an old-time feel to it. Unlike most miniature golf courses built nowadays, each hole has many levels. All those ramps and tunnels make it especially tricky, even for the most seasoned player.

And what holes they are! You'll find Humpty Dumpty, the Statue of Liberty, mermaids, dinosaurs, tree houses, and more. Novelty Golf has two 18-hole courses, a softball batting cage, a baseball batting cage, and an arcade room, so there's plenty for you to do even if you don't like miniature golf. Don't forget to stop by the Bunny Hutch snack bar for a buffalo burger and fries!

⬆ **Kids love this unusual course.**

↗ **This hole has a mermaid statue on top.**

GIDDY GOLFERS MAZE

FINISH

TRASH

START

Try to find a path for your golf ball through this miniature golf maze.

Buildering is the rock-climbing term for the practice of climbing buildings.

THE HIDDEN PEAK

The Chicago area is, well, pretty flat. Very flat, in fact. The closest place to rock climb outdoors is about three hours away! So if you want to do some heavy duty rock climbing in Chicago, you'll have to do it indoors at the Hidden Peak.

If you or your parents have rock-climbing experience, then you'll be allowed to climb the 21-foot-high wall located in the 2,000-square-foot rock-climbing facility. If you're a beginner, then *bouldering* is another option. Bouldering is a type of rock climbing that does not use safety ropes but requires climbing man-made boulders up to where it's still safe to jump or fall off. Your landing is cushioned by 6 inches of rubber surface.

The Hidden Peak offers classes for anyone interested in rock climbing. Their experienced, friendly staff is happy to answer any questions you may have about this popular sport.

⇐ **The climbing wall at Hidden Peak feels almost like the real thing.**

MIXED-UP PICTURE STORY

These pictures should tell a story. But the pictures are all mixed up. Put the pictures in the correct order by filling in the number box in the bottom left-hand corner of each picture.

NIKE TOWN

As soon as you walk into this popular store, you see a life-size sculpture of Michael Jordan. Just a few feet away is a 900-gallon saltwater tank filled with colorful fish and Nike sandals. The nearby "video pool" has eight television sets mounted into the floor showing underwater scenes. Upstairs you'll find signed Michael Jordan basketball sneakers from 1986 through 1995.

And if you decide to buy your own sneakers, you can see them coming up through the "shoot tubes." These long tubes shoot sneakers to the showroom from the stockroom! You may feel as if you've stepped into an episode of *The Jetsons*, which is exactly what the designer of the store, Gordon Thompson III, wanted when he created this space-age store.

⇡ **This Michael Jordan sculpture is true to life.**

While you're at Nike Town, you can compare the size of your feet to Charles Barkley's— he wears a size 15!

Can you fill ⇒ Charles Barkley's shoes?

WHICH TWO ARE THE SAME?

You can get lots of different sneakers at Nike Town. But in this picture there's only one true pair. See if you can find the two that belong together.

PLAYERS WORKSHOP CHILDREN'S THEATRE

Where can you go to see Cinderella, Mark Twain, and Goldilocks? Not as far as you might think! Try the Players Workshop Children's Theatre on Lincoln Park West. All their shows are interactive—at any given moment you might find your self stomping, clapping, singing, or even chanting spells.

This 32-year-old theater group prides itself on its original plays, like "Leaping Lizards Cinderella," "Olivia Twist," "Menumania," and "Ebeneza." Bright costumes and toe-tapping music make each play memorable. And if you're lucky enough to be celebrating a birthday, you can join the actors on stage afterwards for a special birthday celebration. If you crave the bright lights of fame, you can even take acting classes at the "Workshop for Kids."

Many famous actors, such as Bill Murray and George Wendt, had their start at the Players Workshop Children's Theatre.

MY TRAVEL JOURNAL
—That's Entertainment—

These are the names of the places I visited: _____

My favorite place was: _____

The strangest thing I saw was: _____

This is a picture of something I saw

8 LET'S EAT!

WHATEVER FOOD YOU'VE GOT A HANKERING for, Chicago is sure to have it. Feel like biting into an eggroll? Head on over to the restaurants in Chinatown for the best eggrolls anywhere. How about an enchilada? Chicago has many fine Mexican restaurants for you to choose from, especially in the Pilsen area, where colorful murals and Mexican grocery stores line the streets. And if you love Swedish pancakes, have brunch at Anne Sathers in Andersonville, Chicago's Swedish neighborhood.

But of course while you're here you'll have to try a slice of deep dish pizza. Uno's Pizzeria (which Chicagoans call simply Uno's) is where Chicago-style pizza was invented. Chicagoans even have their own style of hot dogs, called, amazingly enough, Chicago-style hot dogs. You can try the best at Superdawg Drive-In.

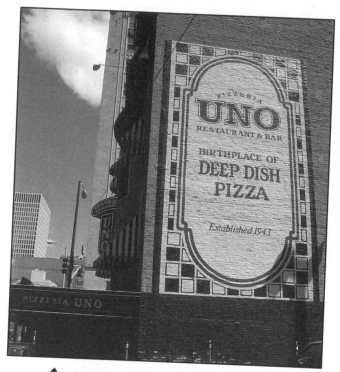

⬆ **Chicago is famous for its pizza.**

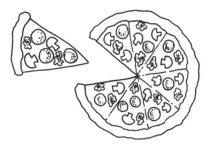

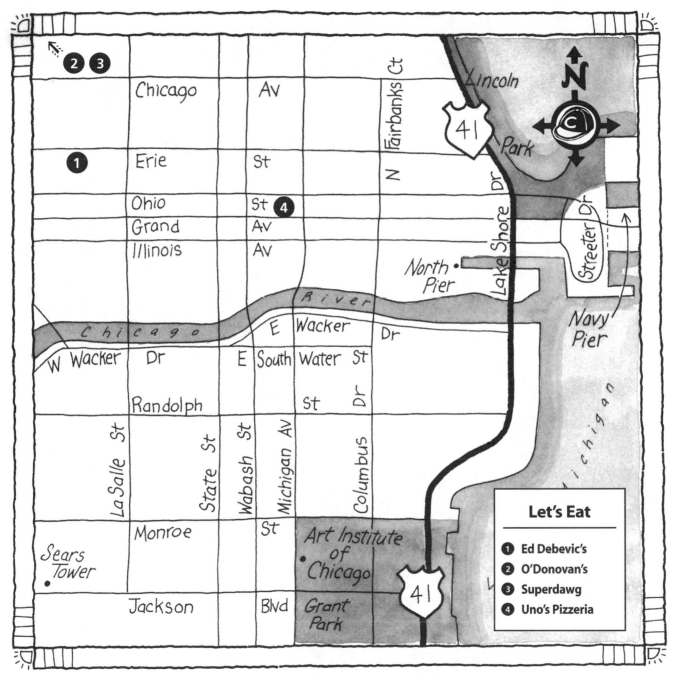

UNO'S PIZZERIA

So what's the big deal about Chicago-style pizza, huh? Isn't pizza just pizza?

Sorry, 'fraid not. Chicago-style pizza means deep dish pizza, the thick gooey pie Chicago is known for. The most famous place to get this kind of pizza is Uno's, the king of deep dish pizza joints and the place where it all began. Be prepared to wait at this bustling pizzeria—folks from all over come for a slice of this world-famous pie.

In 1943 Ike Sewell decided to try something new with his pizza recipe. Instead of making a thin crust, he baked his pizza in a deep pan (which is why deep dish pizza is also called pan pizza) so that the crust was thick. His idea was an instant success. Soon people were lining up to try this new taste sensation. Some say competitors snooped through Uno's garbage to learn the secrets of his flaky crust.

⤒ Uno's Pizzeria is a must.

Two tons of pizza sauce and 8,000 pounds of mozzarella are delivered to Uno's every week.

UNSCRAMBLE THE WORDS

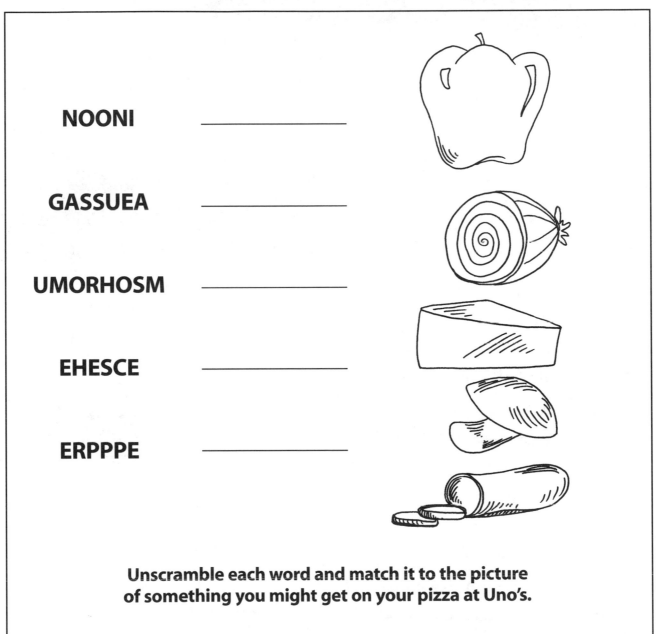

NOONI _____

GASSUEA _____

UMORHOSM _____

EHESCE _____

ERPPPE _____

Unscramble each word and match it to the picture
of something you might get on your pizza at Uno's.

ED DEBEVIC'S

Stepping into Ed Debevic's is like stepping into an honest-to-goodness 1950s diner. Elvis songs are blasting on the jukebox, and neon signs light up every wall. But what Ed's is really known for is the wacky wait staff. You might be served by a waitress dressed in a poodle skirt who suddenly decides to dance on the counter tops. And don't be surprised when your waitperson snaps his or her gum and demands your order impatiently, throwing out wisecracks and insulting everyone at the table. The smart-aleck behavior is all in fun.

⇑ **A lively scene at Ed Debevic's**

You can order meatloaf, mashed potatoes, chiliburgers, milkshakes, fries, malts, and more. While you're waiting for your burger, read the funny signs plastered on the walls—they're sure to make you giggle. If you want to take home a memento from Ed's, check out the souvenir stand, with its pickle pens, T-shirts, and kazoos.

HAPPY DAYS DINER

It's back to the 1950s at Ed Debevic's. Color this old-fashioned scene.

SUPERDAWG DRIVE-IN

New Yorkers, of course, claim that they have the best hot dogs. But anyone who really appreciates red hots knows that Chicago-style dogs are the best. A true Chicago-style hot dog is steamed or boiled and served on a steamed bun with mustard, relish, onion, dill pickle, and tomatoes. And the best place to get a true Chicago-style dog is Superdawg.

In 1948 Maurie Berman and his wife, Florence, started Superdawg, now the only drive-in restaurant in Chicago. When you pull up in your car, the car hop races out to take your order. Once your order is ready, the car hop clips your tray of food onto your car door. This Chicago favorite has been featured in the movie *Sixteen Candles* and the television show *Crime Story*, as well as a bunch of commercials.

It is practically against the law to add catsup to your Chicago-style hot dog!

⬆ **Hot dogs rule the day (and night) at Superdawg.**

SUPERDAWG

How many words can you make from letters in the word
SUPERDAWG? Two words have been found for you.
How many more can you find?

SUPERDAWG

Peas

Sad

O'DONOVAN'S

There's never a boring meal at O'Donovan's, where you can eat a burger with a side order of . . . magic! Once called Schulien's, this old favorite has been around since 1915. That's when Big Matt Schulien decided to try something new by having magic shows at his restaurant. Customers have been enjoying the magic shows on Thursdays and weekend nights ever since. In the evening, a magician strolls from table to table performing his favorite tricks. Where else can you enjoy card, rope, and coin tricks while you eat your french fries?

Let's not forget about the food! O'Donovan's has all kinds of kid-friendly stuff, like buffalo wings, nachos, hamburgers, and brats. Just don't forget the magic words: "More magic, please!"

The most famous magician of all time, Harry Houdini, also had an interest in planes. He was the first person ever to fly a plane in Australia.

⇒ **O'Donovan's is on the corner of Irving Park and Hoyne—literally!**

MY TRAVEL JOURNAL
—Let's Eat!—

My favorite restaurant was: _____

The most unusual food I ate was: _____

My least favorite food was: _____

This is a picture of one restaurant I visited

CALENDAR OF CHICAGO EVENTS

JANUARY

Chicago Boat, Sports, and RV Show

McCormick Place
2300 S. Lake Shore Dr.
(312) 946-6262
This is a great time to check out the latest cool boats and RVs, as well as live entertainment.

Chicago Cubs Fan Convention

Chicago Hilton and Towers,
720 South Michigan
(773) 404-CUBS
Talk baseball with fellow fans and see some of your favorite players and coaches.

FEBRUARY

Azalea Flower Show

Lincoln Park Conservatory
2400 N. Stockton Dr.
(312) 742-7736
Escape the freezing cold with this colorful azalea show that will raise your winter-weary spirits.

Black History Month

Chicago Cultural Center and the DuSable Museum
(773) 947-0600
All month long you'll find special events and activities celebrating African American history.

⚡ **There's year-round fun at Navy Pier.**

Chicago Auto Show

McCormick Place
2300 S. Lake Shore Dr.
(312) 692-2220
Car lovers will go crazy over this annual event featuring new cars and trucks from around the world.

Chinese New Year Parade

Wentworth and Cermak Street
(312) 225-6198
Celebrate the New Year Chinese style with a special parade featuring a fiery dragon.

International Kennel Dog Show

McCormick Place
2300 S. Lake Shore Dr.
(773) 237-5100
The event dog lovers look forward to every year.

The Medinah Shrine Circus

Medinah Temple
600 N. Wabash, (312) 266-5000
This annual circus event runs from the end of February through the first two weeks in March.

MARCH

St. Patrick's Day Parade

Dearborn Street from Wacker
Drive to Van Buren Street,
(312) 744-3370
One of the biggest St. Patrick's
Day parades in the country is
celebrated in Chicago. Be sure
not to miss the kelly green
Chicago River.

APRIL

Cubs Opening Day

Wrigley Field, (773) 404-CUBS
Bring your lucky charm to the
opening day for this poor team.
It just might work.

Greek Independence Day

Halsted Street in Greektown
(312) 744-3315
Even if you're not Greek, you'll
enjoy this parade.

Spring and Easter Show

Lincoln Park Conservatory
2400 N. Stockton Dr.
(773) 294-4700
Gaze at hundreds of colorful
flowers and celebrate spring!

↥ **You can learn how to weave baskets at the Chicago Historical Society.**

White Sox Opening Day

Comisky Park, (312) 674-1000
Bundle up, grab a hot dog, and
root for your favorite team!

MAY

Buckingham Fountain Color Light Show

Grant Park
Chicago's most famous fountain
shoots its colorful sprays every
year from May through
September.

Polish Constitution Day Parade

Dearborn Street from Wacker
Drive to Van Buren Street
(312) 744-3315
There are lots of Poles in
Chicago, and they all show up
for this huge party!

⬆ **Museum of Science and Industry in Hyde Park**

JUNE

Andersonville Midsummer's Fest
Clark Street from Foster to Catalpa, (773) 728-2995
This event is held in the middle of Chicago's Swedish neighborhood.

Chicago Blues Fest
Petrillo Music Shell, Grant Park (312) 744-3315
The blues started right here in Chicago. To hear the best, come to this huge outdoor fest, one of the most popular events all year.

Printers Row Bookfair
Dearborn Street from Harrison to Polk, (312) 987-1980
Open air book market with thousands of used and new books on display.

Puerto Rican Day Parade
Dearborn Street from Wacker Drive to Congress
(312) 744-3315
A festive parade featuring Puerto Rican entertainment and food.

Wells Street Art Fair
1900 N. Lincoln, (312) 337-1938
Lots of sculpture, paintings, jewelry, and more are at this annual art fair.

JULY

Chicago Country Music Festival
Grant Park, (312) 744-3370
Come and enjoy lots of good ol' country music.

Chicago Mackinac Island Boat Race
Starting line at Monroe Street Harbor, (312) 861-7777
Boats of all shapes and sizes race this 300 mile race that runs along the length of Lake Michigan.

Chinatown Summer Fair
Wentworth Avenue between 22nd and 24th Streets
(312) 225-6198
Enjoy this wonderful neighborhood while tasting some of its treats.

Fourth of July Celebration
Grant Park, (312) 744-3315
Fireworks, parades, and more are all a part of this patriotic festival.

Taste of Chicago
Grant Park, (312) 744-3315
A week-long street fair with about 100 Chicago restaurants at booths to show off their favorite dishes. One of Chicago's most famous and popular events.

AUGUST

Bud Billiken Parade
King Drive, (312) 744-3315
Enjoy Chicago's oldest and biggest parade.

Chicago Air and Water Show
North Avenue Beach
(312) 744-3370
Watch Blue Angel fighter pilots soar in their jets in this awesome display of super-fast jets and boats.

Oz Festival
Lincoln Park, (312) 744-3315
Follow the yellow brick road to a wide variety of fun activites.

Teddy Bear Picnic
Brookfield Zoo, (708) 485-0263
Two whole days of teddy bear parades and contests. Be sure to enter your best-loved bear in this annual event.

Venetian Night
From Monroe Harbor to the planetarium, (312) 744-3370
This eagerly awaited parade showcases fancy, brightly lit boats and fireworks.

SEPTEMBER

Chicago's Jazz Fest
Petrillo Music Shell, Grant Park
(312) 744-3315
Another huge outdoor festival that jazz lovers from all over attend annually.

Chicago Labor Day Parade
Dearborn Street from Wacker Drive to Van Buren Street
(312) 744-3315
Watch marching bands and celebrate the coming of fall.

Mexican Independence Day Parade
Dearborn Street from Wacker Drive to Van Buren Street
(312) 744-3315
This colorful parade commemorates Mexico's independence.

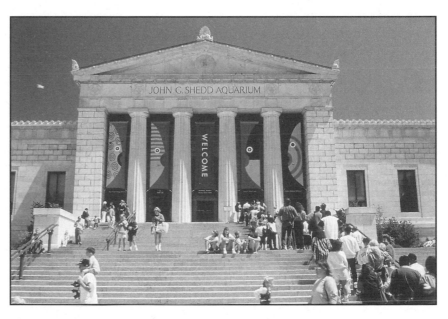

⇡ **The handsome entrance to the Shedd Aquarium**

OCTOBER

The Halloween Happening
State Street, (312) 744-3315
Join thousands of other kids in costumes.

Chicago International Children's Film Festival
Facets Multimedia
1517 W. Fullerton
(773) 281-9075
Eleven days of children's films and videos from 35 countries as well as hands-on workshops and activities.

Chicago Marathon
Starts at Grant Park, Columbus Dr.,(312) 744-3370
Lace up your running shoes and get pumped for this heavy duty marathon.

Columbus Day Parade
Dearborn Street from Wacker Drive to Congress
(312) 744-3370
Lots of food, music, and fun during this annual parade honoring Italian explorer Christopher Columbus.

Spooky Zoo Spectacular
Lincoln Park Zoo
2200 N. Cannon Dr.
(312) 742-2000
Trick or treat with lions and tigers and bears, oh my! Bring your treat bag—the zoo gives out over a million pieces of candy each year.

NOVEMBER

American Indian Center of Chicago Pow Wow
IC Pavillion
1150 W. Harrison
(773) 275-5871
Join hundreds of Native Americans from around the world as they participate in singing, dancing, and craft activities.

Christmas Parade
Michigan Avenue from Balbo to Wacker Drive
(312) 935-8747
A post–Thanksgiving Day parade featuring Santa and the gang.

Holiday Tree Lighting Ceremony
James C. Thompson Center
100 W. Randolph
(312) 814-6660
The 75-foot tree in front of the Thompson Center is lit each year while local choirs sing carols.

DECEMBER

Caroling to the Animals
Lincoln Park Zoo
2200 N. Cannon Dr.
(312) 742-2000
Sing Christmas carols to the residents of Chicago's favorite zoo.

A Christmas Carol
Goodman Theater
200 S. Columbus Dr.
(312) 433-3800
Discover the true meaning of Christmas with this famous play by Charles Dickens.

Nutcracker Ballet
Arie Crown Theater
McCormick Place
(312) 791-6000
Dancing sugar plum fairies and tin soldiers make this ballet a holiday favorite.

RESOURCE GUIDE: WHAT, WHERE, AND WHEN?

Here is a listing of the places mentioned in this book, plus others in and around Chicago of interest to children and families. The information in this Resource Guide changes often, so call before you go.

If You Get Lost

It's a good idea to make a plan with your parents about what to do if you lose them. If you get lost while you're visiting Chicago, go to a uniformed park ranger or police officer. If you're in a store or restaurant, go to the person working behind the cash register. If you're outside and don't see a ranger or police officer, find a mother with children and tell her you're lost.

In an emergency, you can dial 911 from any phone. You won't need money to do this, even at a pay phone. Only dial 911 if you need the police, the fire department, or an ambulance.

Important Phone Numbers
Injury, accident, or emergency, 911
Chicago Police, (312) 746-6000
Poison Control, (800) 942- 5969
Fire Department, (312) 744-6666
Highway Patrol, (312) 603-7736

Visitor Information
Chicago Office of Tourism, 806 N. Michigan Ave., (312) 744-2400 or (800) 487-2448

Chicago Cultural Center, 78 E. Washington St., (312) 744-2400 or (800) 487-2446

Transportation
Car Rentals
Avis, (800) 331-1212
Budget, (773) 686-6800
Enterprise, (800) 736-8222

⬆ **The "El" train is good way to get around Chicago.**

Public Transportation
Chicago Transit Authority, (312) 836-7000
Continental Air Transport Express Bus, (312) 454-7800
Greyhound, (800) 231-2222
Midway Airport, (773) 767-0500
O'Hare International Airport, (773) 686-2200

Taxis
Flash Cab, (773) 561-1444
Yellow Cab, (312) 829-4222

Tours
American Sightseeing Tours,
  (312) 251-3100
Odyssey Cruises, (630) 990-0800

Attractions
Adler Planetarium, 1300 S.
Lake Shore Dr., (312) 322-0300.
Open daily 9–5, Fridays to 9,
Saturday and Sunday to 6.
During the summer weekday
hours are extended. Closed
Thanksgiving and Christmas.

**ARTIFACT Center at Spertus
Museum**, Spertus Institute of
Jewish Studies, 618 S. Michigan
Ave., (312) 322-1754. Open
Sunday through Thursday
1–4:30 p.m.

Art Institute of Chicago, 111 S.
Michigan Ave., (312) 443-3500.
Open Monday, Wednesday,
Thursday, and Friday 10:30–4:30,
Tuesdays 10:30–8, Saturday
10–5, Sundays noon to 5.

Brookfield Zoo, Chicago
Zoological Society, 3300 Golf
Rd., Brookfield, (708) 485-0263.
Open daily Memorial Day to
Labor Day 9:30–6, rest of the
year 10–5.

Buckingham Fountain, Grant
Park near Congress Parkway.

Chicago Bears, Soldier Field,
425 East McFetridge Dr., (847)
615-2327. Season runs from
August to January.

Chicago Blackhawks, United
Center, 1901 W. Madison St.,
(312) 455-7000. Season runs
from October to mid-April.

Chicago Botanic Garden, Lake
Cook Road, Glencoe, (847) 835-
5440. Open daily 8 a.m. to
sunset. Closed Christmas.

Chicago Bulls, United Center,
1901 W. Madison St., (312) 455-
4000. Season runs from
November to mid-April.

Chicago Children's Museum,
Navy Pier, 700 E. Grand Ave.,
(312) 527-1000. Open Memorial
Day through Labor Day Monday
through Sunday 10–5, rest of the
year Tuesday through Sunday
10–5.

⇡ **What do you think these kids are doing? You can find out at
the Adler Planetarium.**

Chicago Cubs, Wrigley Field, 1060 W. Addison St., (773) 404-2827 for schedule, (312) 831-CUBS for tickets in Illinois, (800) 347-CUBS for tickets outside Illinois. Season runs from April through September.

Chicago Cultural Center, 78 E. Washington St., (312) 744-6630 (Chicago Department of Cultural Affairs) or (312) 346-3278 (Programs and Exhibitions). Open Monday through Wednesday 9–7, Thursday 9–9, Friday 9–6, Saturday 9–5, Sunday 11–5. Closed holidays.

Chicago Historical Society, Clark Street at North Avenue, (312) 642-4600. Open Monday through Saturday 9:30–4:30, Sunday noon to 5.

⇡ **Wrigley Field is a great place to see a ball game.**

Chicago White Sox, Comiskey Park, 333 W. 35th St., (312) 924-1000 for schedule; (312) 831-1769 for tickets. Season runs from April through September.

Doggy Beach, between Belmont and Irving Park Road.

DuSable Museum of African American History, 740 E. 56th Place, (773) 947-0600. Open Monday through Saturday 10–5, Sunday 12–5. Closed New Year's Day, Easter, Independence Day, Thanksgiving, and Christmas.

Ed Debevic's, 640 N. Wells, (312) 664-1707. Open Sunday through Thursday 11 a.m.– 9 p.m., Friday and Saturday 11–midnight.

Field Museum of Natural History, 1400 S. Lake Shore Drive, (312) 922-9410. Open daily 9–5. Closed New Year's Day and Christmas.

Garfield Park Conservatory, 300 N. Central Park Blvd., (312) 746-5100. Open daily 9–5.

↑ **Kids playing in a sprinkler at the Indian Boundary Zoo**

Grant Park, East Randolph Street to East McFetridge Drive at Lake Michigan, (312) 747-2200.

Harold Washington Library, 400 S. State St., (312) 747-4200. Open Monday, Wednesday, Friday, and Saturday 9–5; Tuesday and Thursday 11–7, Sunday 1–5. Closed holidays.

Hard Rock Café Chicago, 63 W. Ontario, (312) 943-2252. Open

Monday through Thursday 11:30 a.m.–11 p.m., Friday 11:30 a.m.–11:30 p.m., Saturday 11 a.m. to midnight, Sunday 11:30 a.m.–10 p.m. Closed Christmas and Thanksgiving.

Hidden Peak, Lakeshore Academy, 937 W. Chestnut St., (312) 563-9400. Open Monday through Friday 12–2p.m. and 5–9 p.m., Saturday and Sunday noon to 6.

Indian Boundary Zoo, 2500 W. Lunt St., (312) 742-7887. Open daily 9–4.

John G. Shedd Aquarium, 1200 S. Lake Shore Dr., (312) 939-2438. September 2 through May 25, 9–5, May 26 through September 1, 9–6.

John Hancock Center Observatory, 875 N. Michigan Ave., (312) 751-3681. Open daily 9 a.m. to midnight.

Kohl Children's Museum, 165 Green Bay Rd., Wilmette, (847) 256-6056. Open Monday 9–12, Tuesday through Saturday 9–5, Sunday 12–5.

Lincoln Park Conservatory, Lincoln Park, 2400 N. Stockton Dr., (312) 742-7736. Open daily 9–5.

Lincoln Park Zoo, 2200 N. Cannon Dr., (312) 742-2000. Open daily 9–5.

Mexican Fine Arts Center, 1852 W. 19th St., (312) 738-1503. Open Tuesday through Sunday 10–5. Closed Monday and New Year's Day, Memorial

↑ **An elephant at Novelty Golf**

Day, Independence Day, Labor Day, Thanksgiving Day, and Christmas Day.

Museum of Broadcast Communications, Chicago Cultural Center, Michigan Avenue at Washington Street, (312) 629-6000. Open Monday through Saturday 10–4:30, Sunday noon to 5.

Museum of Contemporary Art, 220 E. Chicago Ave., (312) 280-2660. Open Tuesday 10–8, Wednesday through Sunday 10–5. Closed Monday, New Year's Day, Thanksgiving, and Christmas.

Museum of Holography, 1134 W. Washington Blvd., (312) 226-1007. Open Wednesday through Sunday 12:30–5.

Museum of Science and Industry, 57th Street and Lake Shore Drive, (773) 684-1414. Open daily Memorial Day to Labor Day 9:30–5:30; rest of the year Monday through Friday 9:30–4, Saturday and Sunday 9:30–5:30. Closed Christmas.

↟ **Buckingham Fountain makes quite a splash.**

Nature Museum of the Chicago Academy of Sciences, (773) 549-0606. Call for information about exhibits throughout the Chicago area.

Navy Pier, 600 E. Grand Ave., (312) 791-7437. Open Monday through Friday 6 a.m.–8 p.m., weekends 6 a.m.–10 p.m. In summer: Monday through Friday 6 a.m.–10 p.m., weekends 6 a.m.–midnight.

Nike Town, 669 N. Michigan Ave., (312) 642-6363. Open Monday through Friday 10–8, Saturday 9:30–7, Sunday 11–6.

Noble Horse Equestrian Center, 1410 N. Orleans St., (312) 266-7878. Open Monday through Friday 9–9, Saturday and Sunday 9–7.

North Park Village Nature Center, 5801 N. Pulaski Rd., (312) 744-5472. Open daily 10–4. Closed some holidays.

North Pier, 435 E. Illinois St., (312) 836-4300. Open Monday through Thursday 11–7, Friday and Saturday 11–8, Sunday 11–6.

⬆ **Jean Dubuffet's**
Monument with Standing
Beast, **outside the**
Thompson Center

Novelty Golf, 3640 W. Devon Ave., Lincolnwood, (847) 679-9434. Open from April through mid-October daily 10 a.m. to midnight.

Oak Street Beach, Oak Street and Lake Shore Drive, (312) 747-0832. Open Memorial Day through mid-September daily 9–9.

O'Donovan's, 2100 W. Irving Park Road, (773) 478-2100. Monday 4 p.m.–2 a.m., Tuesday–Friday 11 a.m.–2 a.m., Saturday 11 a.m.–3 a.m., Sunday 10 a.m.–2 a.m.

Oriental Institute, University of Chicago, 1155 E. 58th St., (773) 702-9520. Open Tuesday through Saturday 10–4, Sunday noon to 4, open until 8:30 on Wednesday.

Oz Park, Webster Avenue and Larrabee Street at Lincoln Avenue, (312) 742-7898.

Peace Museum, 350 W. Ontario, fourth floor, (312) 440-1860. Open Tuesday through Saturday 11–5. Closed major holidays.

Players Workshop Children's Theatre, Lincoln Park Cultural Center, 2045 Lincoln Park West, (773) 929-6288. Shows are at 2 p.m. on Sunday.

Rock 'n' Roll McDonalds, 600 N. Clark St., (312) 664-7940. Open 24 hours a day 365 days a year.

Rosehill Cemetery, 5800 N. Ravenswood Ave., (773) 561-5940. Open Monday–Saturday 8–5; Sunday 10–4. Guided tours offered the first and third Saturday of every month at 10 a.m., weather permitting.

Sears Tower Skydeck, Jackson Boulevard between Franklin Street and Wacker Drive, (312) 875-9696. Open daily March through Sept. 9 a.m.–11 p.m., October through Feb. 10–10.

Six Flags Great America Amusement Park, 542 N. Route 21, Gurnee, (847) 249-2133. Call for hours.

Skate on State, State Street between Washington and Randolph Streets, (312) 744-3315. Open late November through late February 9 a.m.–7:15 p.m. Skate rental available.

Superdawg Drive-In, 6363 N. Milwaukee Ave., (773) 763-0660. Open Sunday through Thursday 11 a.m.–1 a.m., Friday and Saturday 11 a.m.–2 a.m.

Terra Museum of American Art, 664 N. Michigan Ave., (312) 664-3939. Open Tuesday 10–8, Wednesday through Saturday 10–6, Sunday noon to 5. Closed Monday.

Thompson Center, 100 W. Randolph St., (312) 814-6667. Open Monday through Saturday 8:30–5. Closed Sunday and state holidays.

Uno's Pizzeria, 29 E. Ohio, (312) 321-1000. Open Monday through Friday 11:30 a.m.–1 a.m., Saturday 11:30 a.m.–2 a.m., Sunday 11:30 a.m.–11:30 p.m.

Untitled Picasso, Daley Civic Center, 50 W. Washington St.

Untouchables Tour, (773) 881-1195.

USA Rainbo Roller Skating Center, 4836 N. Clark St., (773) 271-5668. Call for hours.

Water Tower, 806 N. Michigan Ave., (312) 744-2400 or (800) 487-2448. Open daily 9:30–5. Closed holidays.

ANSWERS TO PUZZLES

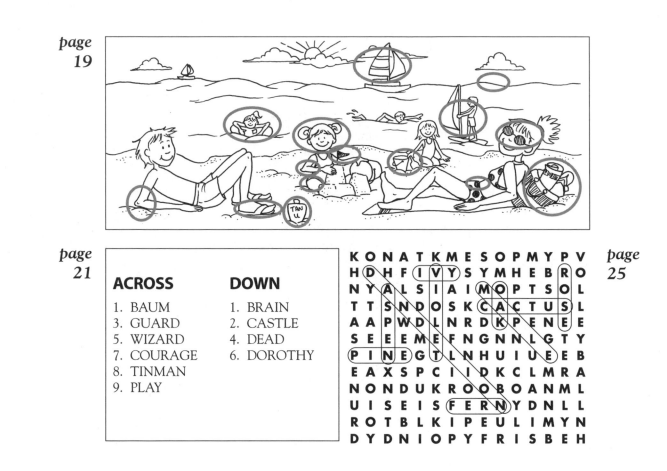

page 19

page 21

ACROSS	DOWN
1. BAUM	1. BRAIN
3. GUARD	2. CASTLE
5. WIZARD	4. DEAD
7. COURAGE	6. DOROTHY
8. TINMAN	
9. PLAY	

page 25

```
K O N A T K M E S O P M Y P V
H D H F I V Y S Y M H E B R O
N Y A L S I A I M O P T S O L
T T S N D O S K C A C T U S L
A A P W D L N R D K P E N E E
S E E E M E F N G N N L G T Y
P I N E G T L N H U I U E E B
E A X S P C I I D K C L M R A
N O N D U K R O O B O A N M L
U I S E I S F E R N Y D N L L
R O T B L K I P E U L I M Y N
D Y D N I O P Y F R I S B E H
```

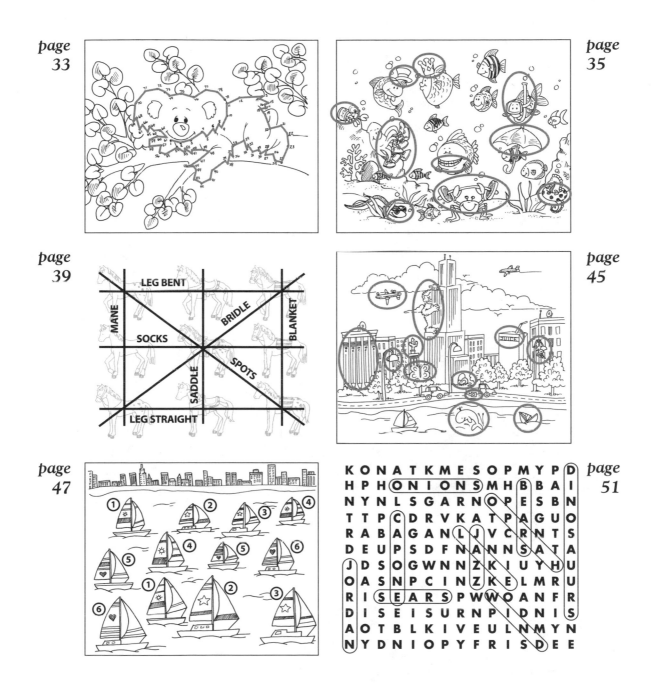

page 33

page 35

page 39

LEG BENT
MANE
BRIDLE
BLANKET
SOCKS
SADDLE
SPOTS
LEG STRAIGHT

page 45

page 47

page 51

K O N A T K M E S O P M Y P D
H P H O N I O N S M H B B A I
N Y N L S G A R N O P E S B N
T T P C D R V K A T P A G U O
R A B A G A N L J V C R N T S
D E U P S D F N A N N S A T A
J D S O G W N N Z K I U Y H U
O A S N P C I N Z K E L M R R
R I S E A R S P W W O A N F S
D S E I S U R N P I D N I S
A O T B L K I V E U L N M Y N
N Y D N I O P Y F R I S D E E

page 53

page 55

page 65

page 67

page 69

page
75

page
77

page
79

page
81

page
85

ACROSS

5. PIONEER
6. FORT
7. MOVIE
8. WATCH
9. WALL

DOWN

1. CHICAGO
2. PEOPLE
3. CRAFTS
4. HISTORICAL

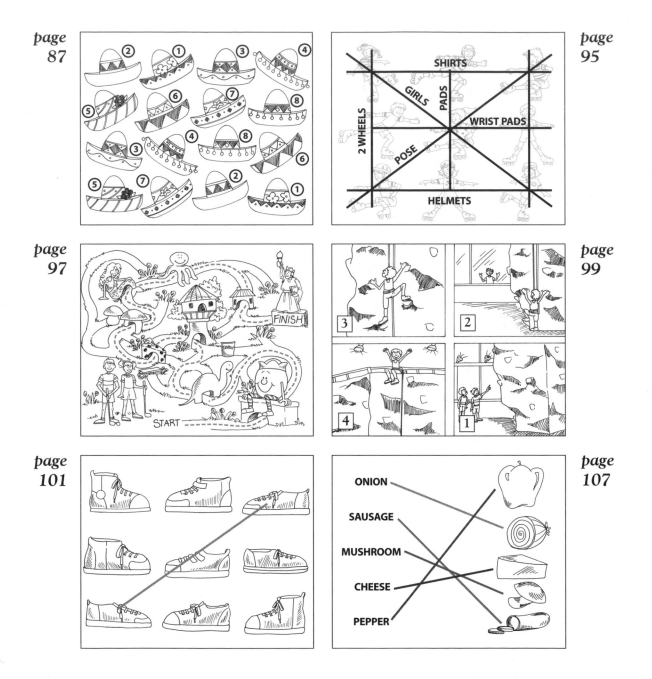

GEOGRAPHICAL INDEX
WHERE IS EVERYTHING?

INDEX

Guidebooks *that* really *guide*

City•Smart™ Guidebooks

Pick one for your favorite city: *Albuquerque, Anchorage, Austin, Calgary, Charlotte, Chicago, Cincinnati, Cleveland, Denver, Indianapolis, Kansas City, Memphis, Milwaukee, Minneapolis/St. Paul, Nashville, Pittsburgh, Portland, Richmond, Salt Lake City, San Antonio, San Francisco, St. Louis, Tampa/St. Petersburg, Tucson.* US \$12.95 to 15.95

Retirement & Relocation Guidebooks

The World's Top Retirement Havens, Live Well in Honduras, Live Well in Ireland, Live Well in Mexico. US \$15.95 to \$16.95

Travel•Smart® Guidebooks

Trip planners with select recommendations to *Alaska, American Southwest, Arizona, Carolinas, Colorado, Deep South, Eastern Canada, Florida, Florida Gulf Coast, Hawaii, Illinois/Indiana, Kentucky/Tennessee, Maryland/Delaware, Michigan, Minnesota/Wisconsin, Montana/Wyoming/Idaho, New England, New Mexico, New York State, Northern California, Ohio, Pacific Northwest, Pennsylvania/New Jersey, South Florida and the Keys, Southern California, Texas, Utah, Virginias, Western Canada.* US \$14.95 to \$17.95

Rick Steves' Guides

See *Europe Through the Back Door* and take along guides to *France, Belgium & the Netherlands; Germany, Austria & Switzerland; Great Britain & Ireland; Italy; Scandinavia; Spain & Portugal; London; Paris;* or *Best of Europe.* US \$12.95 to \$21.95

Adventures in Nature

Plan your next adventure in *Alaska, Belize, Caribbean, Costa Rica, Guatemala, Hawaii, Honduras, Mexico.* US \$17.95 to \$18.95

Into the Heart of Jerusalem

A traveler's guide to visits, celebrations, and sojourns. US \$17.95

The People's Guide to Mexico

This is so much more than a guidebook—it's a trip to Mexico in and of itself, complete with the flavor of the country and its sights, sounds, and people. US \$22.95

JOHN MUIR PUBLICATIONS
A DIVISION OF AVALON TRAVEL PUBLISHING
5855 Beaudry Street, Emeryville, CA 94608

Please check our web site at www.travelmatters.com for current prices and editions, or see your local bookseller.

Cater Your Interests on Your Next Vacation